PRAISE FOR "ICARUS SYNDROME"

"John Long is a genre unto himself. Few other writers can match his lean and unpredictable prose, and this latest collection proves that he remains a shrewd witness of today's cutting-edge adventure sports."

Andrew Bisharat
Climber
National Geographic Writer

"Adventure and climbing legend John Long is an oddity, 'cause not many adventurers can write, and not many writers can climb, kayak, etc. John Long's *Icarus Syndrome* is a colorful brew of adventurers, heroes and misfits, and John writes about them with a curiously muscular, effortless literary style to impart such sensitive insights."

Steve Schwartz
Producer for *The Road, The Counselor, All the Old Knives,* and president of Chockstone Pictures

"*Icarus* is John Long's howl of praise for the excesses and triumphs of meteoric youth. In these deft autobiographical sketches, spangled with his gift for the mordant phrase, Long evokes all the sense of living life to the hilt that infuses the writings of one of America's greatest practitioners of the art."

David Roberts
author of *The Mountain of My Fear, The Bears Ears: A Human History,* and other books

"John Long makes me sick with envy. I mean, how a futuristic ultra-elite-athlete became a truly accomplished writer of literary adventure stories delivering complex emotions and characters alongside throat-grabbing thrills is, well, nothing short of miraculous."

Daniel Duane
Men's Journal

These tales flow like honey down the edge of a knife. One side of the blade is love and the other is death, and that describes the central preoccupations of this volume. John Long is at the top of his game — a master storyteller.

Jeff Jackson
At Large Editor, *Climbing Magazine*
Prof. of Literature, University of Hawaii, Maui

Anyone interested in getting out beyond the ordinary, and, say, crew onto a black-smoke-spewing barge headed up a nameless Brazilian river in search of the existential headwaters, owes it to themselves to get a copy of Icarus Syndrome. Stories like "A Bend in the River" are simply all time.

Duane Raleigh
Editor and Chief, *Outside Magazine Group*

ICARUS SYNDROME

CATHARSIS

John Long

Icarus Syndrome is published under Catharsis Books, a sectionalized division under Di Angelo Publications, INC.

CATHARSIS BOOKS

an imprint of Di Angelo Publications.

Printed in United States of America

Di Angelo Publications
4265 San Felipe #1100
Houston, Texas 77027
www. diangelopublications.com

Library of Congress Registration Hardback
Icarus Syndrome
ISBN:978-1-942549-83-3
First Edition - Printed in the United States of America

Downloadable via Kindle, iBooks and NOOK.

Words: John Long
Cover Design: Savina Deianova
Cover Illustrator: Alyse Dietel
Interior Design: Kimberly James
Editors: Cody Wootton, Ashley Crantas

Downloadable via Kindle, iBooks and NOOK.

1. Biography & Autobiography --- Personal Memoirs
2. Travel --- Special Interest --- Adventure
3. Sports & Recreation --- Extreme Sports

United States of America with int. distribution.

Cover Illustration by Alyse Dietel

www.amilliontinylines.com

@amilliontinylines

A Million Tiny Lines

FOREWORD

Never would I have imagined that I, a kid who grew up on the tundra of southwest Alaska, would be shouldered with the honor of writing a foreword for a book written by someone I'd grown up reading about, someone as legendary as John Long. To be completely honest — being forward for this foreword — what you're about to read needs no introduction. I don't think one could adequately introduce the stories contained herein. Perhaps what would serve this book better than a foreword is a warning. Yes. That is what I've been tasked to write. A warning.

Warning: What you're about to read, Icarus Syndrome, is not what you're expecting, or emotionally prepared for. Yes, there will be the blood-pounding, bone-crushing action, taut-rope cliff-side thrills one might come to expect from a man who has spent his existence pushing earthly boundaries. The unexpected is what you need to be forewarned of, because this book is so much more than the usual tough guy memoir of gritty I-did-this stories. You're about to get crushed beneath an avalanche of emotion. The weight of these stories from John's life will overwhelm you with the varied nuance and beauty of a million individual snowflakes; a weight that will at times take your breath away, from profound loss of climbing partners and dear friends to brushes with legends of the mountains, the sea, and even the rodeo ring.

The warnings don't stop there.

Be warned that you will laugh. You will most certainly wince. Old injuries will ache a bit. Your heart will be stirred for loves lost and found. Your own memories of childhood and adolescence will be rekindled. And if modern society hasn't already stripped the humanity from you, you'll likely shed a tear or two.

Those of us who seek adventure, or have tried to quench that thirst and aren't yet satisfied, be warned that you're about to be taken on a journey that will reveal many truths of that search. All revealed through a humbled voice of an individual whose path in life has more twists and turns than a meandering tundra stream. The wisdom John passes on to us here is timeless, and invaluable. He does this by examining his own flaws through the lens of his life, and reveals simple and beautiful truths like, "my ostrich-like avoidance of my own feelings kept me a stranger from myself."

In turn, we get to examine our own lives, as he shares how his "strongest sense of meaning was derived from flying too close to the sun," knowing he could die. He admits, "Logically, it only makes sense to play it safe, stretch out the life we do have," but then admits, "that's never worked out for me." Fortunately for us, John survived to deftly deliver these tales and, in doing so, provides with us a way to recognize the aspects that make us human, that connect us and bind us to each other and our planet.

So, be warned! What you are about to read will not just entertain you—yes, it will certainly do that—but even better, this collection of John Long's stories come together in a tightly woven and gorgeous mosaic of masterful writing and as-good-as-it-gets storytelling. Like some sort of literary El Capitan, Icarus Syndrome, is a memorable work that, by my estimate, rises to the top as some of the best non-fiction I've ever read. I won't forget these stories, and I'd wager a good pair of your wax wings that you won't either.

Don Rearden
author of *The Raven's Gift* and *Without A Paddle*
Bear Valley, Alaska

TABLE OF CONTENTS

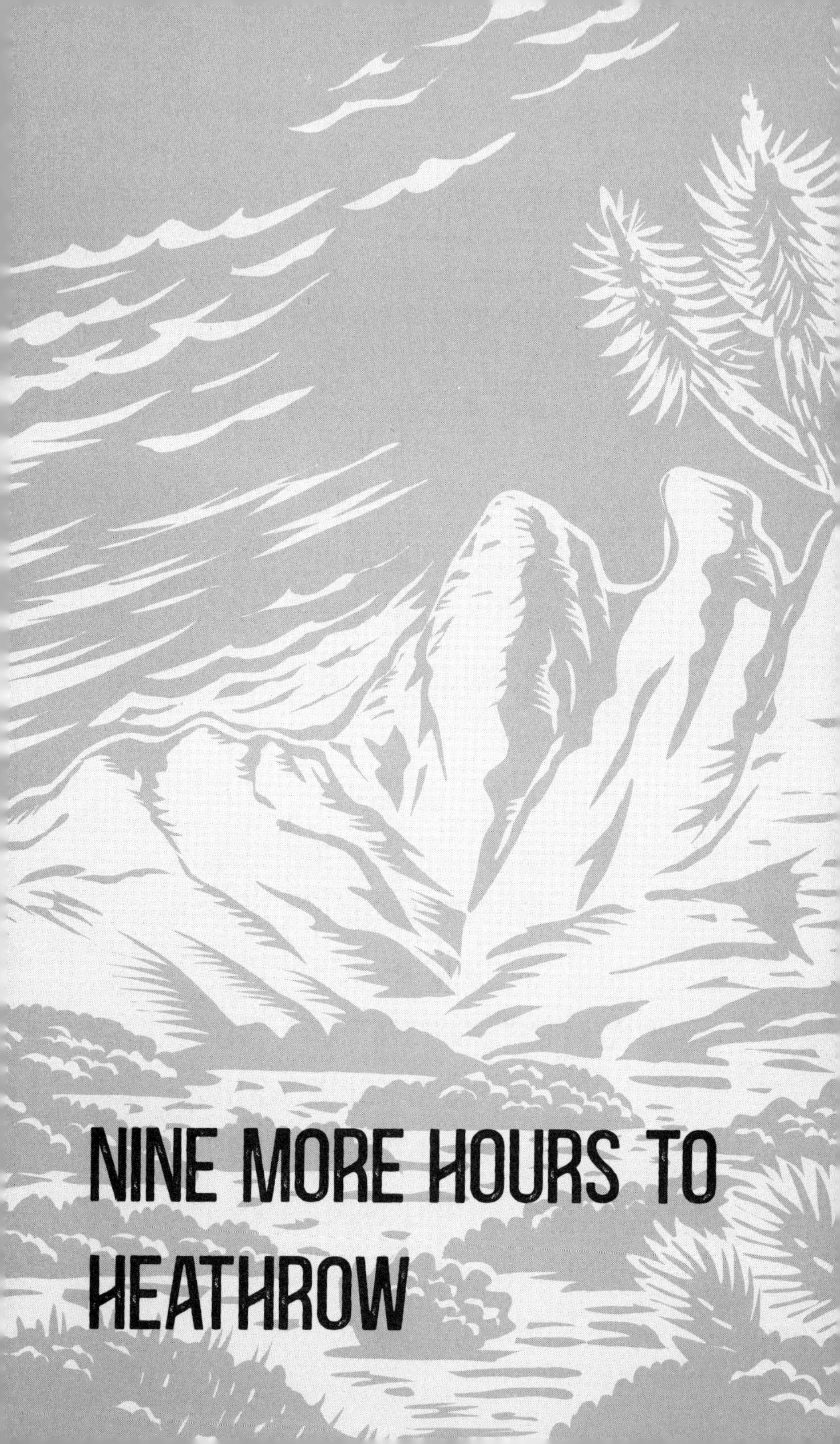

NINE MORE HOURS TO HEATHROW

SHE WAS THE ONLY PERSON sitting in first class, coiled in a window seat. I glimpsed her coming out of the bathroom stall up front, behind the pilot's cabin. When I paused in the aisle and she glanced over with her rowdy green eyes, I knew that was her—which was impossible because she was dead.

I could picture it all from the moment we found her. And hear her voice, frank as rain, how she'd probe us with questions and grab arms till she heard a true answer. I remembered her tattoo, barely visible under the reading light—a thin black line circling her wrist, like a delicate bracelet inked on, with a small heart stenciled in the middle. And I could still see her face as she'd died. I'd watched it happen. I dropped into the aisle seat, and she gazed out the window at nothing. It was ten p.m. and pitch-black outside.

"Eight or nine years ago," I said, "a woman tumbled off the Yosemite Falls trail and got banged up, and we carried her down in a litter. Her name was Hope."

She turned from the window, uncoiling a little in her seat. "I wasn't sure if you were you, or some creeper. Thanks for remembering my name." She reached out her hand and I shook it, and she held on for one moment longer, in that way which changes everything. "You'd climbed one of the big rocks and got all sunburned and had white stuff on your face."

"Zinc oxide."

Hope smiled and said, "You looked like a radish with frosting on it."

She could say wonky things and somehow make them sound normal. "It's crazy you remembered that," I said.

"Who really forgets anything?"

Hope sipped a little wine from a champagne flute sitting on her tray table, and I imagined her springing back from the other side, straight into a SoHo loft full of cubist drawings and Kutani ware. She jumped straight into everything. No brakes. No filters.

"What about Bama?" she asked. "How he got all tweaky and kept fussing over me like Uriah Heep. And the muscley guy. The med student."

"Chet," I said. "He's a doctor now. Up in Vancouver. He thought you were leaking inside."

She hiked up her shirt, exposing a thin red scar rising off her belly button and over her stomach. "My spleen. They took it."

"Ouch," I said, and I clutched my belly. "I went back to school a couple days after the rescue, and never heard back about you. I thought you were gone."

"Three times," she said. She'd twice been resuscitated in the helicopter, doctors had told her, and once more in the ER, where they transfused her with everything they had. She pressed her palms together, giving thanks. She talked a little more about battling back, how sometimes her knee hurt at night, her words coming slower and slower. She had bruises on those memories.

"You seem OK now," I said. "Better than I remember, and you looked good then—till the end."

She shrugged and said, “Well, I’m sorta rich and sorta famous these days.”

“Congratulations.”

She threw her head back and laughed. “Don’t even act like you’re impressed by that.” She grabbed the wine but didn’t drink it. “I’m allergic to lies,” she said. “And I’m living one. I come clean with myself by the time we land at Heathrow, or I walk off this plane in rags.” She wasn’t Cinderella. She was buzzed on Pinot blanc, and so thrown open and bombs away, sitting next to her felt like camping in an avalanche zone.

“So, what about you and your wingman, Bama?” she said. “You couldn’t even look at each other.”

“How’d you remember *that*?”

She cracked a wintry smile, like I’d asked the stupidest question.

“Bouncing down the trail in the litter, there was lightning between you two. With me stuck in the middle, remember?”

“Pretty much,” I said.

“I asked Bama what happened between you, and he lied and said nothing happened. So did you. Remember that too, Sunburn?”

There was laughter in her. And her razing felt like summer. But I had good reason to say nothing. I stood, and she took my arm.

“If you ever sort yourself out, tell me how you did it.” She grabbed her wine and chuckled again, but the flight attendant frowned as he pushed the cart past us and saw me homesteading in first class.

"Just leaving," I told the attendant. I glanced past Hope, not at her, and said, "Glad you made it, Hope."

I hustled to the way-back, found an empty row and crawled into the window seat. Nine more hours to Heathrow. Bama ghosted in and lowered into the aisle seat, all hate and grimace, like he was sitting on a stove. No telling where Bama had actually run off to—I'd only caught the rumors—but I could sense a presence: Bama stewing with the intensity of a thousand suns. Hope was the second person we'd lost on a rescue, both in the same month, and some intangible thing had flown from our lives and we could never call it back. That was my last full season climbing in the valley, my last rescue, and I hadn't seen Bama till now. What Hope said: We never forget anything.

Bama kept blazing up the trail till he collapsed in the dirt at the elbow of a switchback. As soon as we caught him, he wanted to push on. An hour before, Ranger Reggie (the only name he'd answer to) swung by Camp 4—where all the climbers stayed, including us on the rescue team—and grabbed Chet and me. We were smoking hand-rolled cigarettes and holding down a picnic table, peering through the pines at ragged flocks of birds. They were flying high, at rim-level, and heading south. It was last

August, and our spring was gone, and our summer. The few of us still slumming in camp were running on fumes after three months climbing in the valley. But we couldn't leave Mecca till college started in a couple days. Even the birds knew better than to hang around. Served us right we got fetched for a rescue. We had to go. And we had to hit the Falls Trail, said Ranger Reggie. Full speed. Immediately.

We finally caught Bama, a mile above the trailhead, and we all doubled over, sucking air. All Bama said was that a hiker had skidded off the steep part of the trail, right below the rim, and she'd gotten scraped up.

"Well, hell," said Chet. Why kill ourselves, he wanted to know, sprinting after some hiker with a couple measly scrapes?

"The Juniors radioed down she blew out her knee," said Bama, annoyed, "so she can't hike out on her own."

"So we're schlepping her down?" I asked, cringing at the thought.

"You wanna try that shit in the dark?" said Ranger Reggie. "On this trail?"

I scanned across the rubbly north wall above us, and the narrow trail slashing across it in a ragged series of Z's. We'd never get the woman down this trail before dark. Bama shot off again. The trail steepened just above.

"What gives with Bama?" asked Chet, wobbling to his feet.

"He's a hick with a badge," said Reggie. Like we didn't know that. Reggie threw on his daypack and trudged off.

Reggie always got along with us climbers better than he did with fellow rangers. For a hundred reasons.

We charged on, chasing Bama. The last heat of summer hung on us like a cloud without rain. After plowing up the initial slope, we cut across a ledge system, dunking our heads in a streamlet that pooled on the trail. Just above, the trail hooked left and climbed a ramp angling across a bushy granite wall. Then up through a maze of shale inclines and tiered rubble. A few hikers stumbled past, all rubber legs and sunburnt faces.

The rusty sign at the trailhead read: FOR ADVANCED HIKERS ONLY. Every day from May through September, hundreds tried living up to that sign. The Falls Trail rises 3,200 feet in a little over three miles and feels like climbing the stairs to the top of the One World Trade Center. Twice.

Out right and far above, Yosemite Falls pours through a cleft and straight off the north rim, free-falling into a bridal veil. Every summer day, down on the valley floor, thousands march a quarter mile up a paved access road toward the base of the gusher and get soaked to the bone, watching the white cascade. It seems to stretch out a hand to you. Miwok legend says when a tribal member approaches death, their souls travel to the foggy granite slabs below the falls, which locals call the Lost World, where swirling mist and water, streaming over stone, heal their wounds and their memories.

We jogged across the ramp and swarmed up the last 1,000 feet of elevation, covering about a mile over increasingly loose terrain. These final switchbacks formed an invisible barrier against everything below, and all that level ground represented. For anyone, at any time, the way could crumble underfoot. At 7,000 feet elevation, it took us a minute to catch our breaths and debrief the two Juniors—ranger interns—who Bama had sent ahead to fetch the litter chained to the footbridge on the rim.

The Juniors had loaded Hope into the litter, and she kept apologizing for causing all this trouble. Her left knee was red and swollen and she had some scrapes that the Juniors had dressed. She'd tumbled off the crumbling upper switchbacks and, with no secure place to put her, we could only cram together in a single file. Hope and her litter balanced on steep rubble. Bama eyed the queue piling above us, which snaked all the way up to the rim. Nobody could hike past till we got Hope to a clearing half a mile below.

"We best get you to lower ground," said Bama. "Then we regroup."

Hope's eyes settled curiously on Bama, tall and thin as a rake, with his wiry red hair and Baby Jesus face. Add in the plantation accent—leaning towards a higher register—and his tense decorum around women, and no wonder people felt they were meeting the Spider from Mars. Not Hope, who grabbed Bama's hand and said, "Thank you, sir."

"You're very welcome, ma'am," he said, as the worry lines between his eyes relaxed. "Now, let's get you outta here."

We scanned the switchbacks cutting across the hillside. On solid ground we could take turns and piggyback

Hope down, but the gravel, shale, and narrow trail made a fireman's carry too dicey. Chet mumbled out, "The toboggan from hell." Everyone groaned as we stared at the trail, trying to picture something before us that wasn't there: four people carrying a woman across a crumbling balance beam. This could quickly go way wrong, but that was a problem for the future, and the future never felt real to me.

"I'll take the front," said Reggie. He'd suffer, which he liked.

I pulled on my climbing harness. Chet pulled a long nylon sling from the gear pack, tied it with two hand loops at four-foot intervals and clipped the sling into the back of my harness. Hope's eyes closely followed our moves, but we couldn't explain with a hundred hikers bottlenecked behind us. If only she knew.

The litter described a shallow, stretcher-like basket. Hope lay lashed inside it, face up. A thin, aluminum rail ran around a wire mesh bed, contoured for a human body. We'd normally carry this litter with six people, two on each side, one up front and one in back. But not on a trail barely a foot wide, with no room on the sides for the carry. A couple years later, they started making litters with a single wheel and an all-terrain tire mounted below the basket. We could have used one.

Bama reached into his day pack and fetched a small thermos of jet black coffee. We each took a shot, which committed us to get going. We double- and triple-checked everything that might separate us from the accident report. I grabbed the rear rail. Bama and Chet locked their wrists through the hand loops on the sling coming off the back of my harness. Reggie, facing forward, squatted and grabbed the aluminum rail with his hands matched behind his waist. Soon as we hoisted the litter, the weight nose-dived onto Reggie's hands, thickly calloused from hard service. But the shock load nearly buckled his legs as he plowed across the steep trail, heels digging into the loose-packed rubble, the three of us behind getting dragged down the slope like we were tethered to a runaway horse.

Lying powerless in a litter made wimps out of El Cap speed climbers, but Hope owned it. Even when we'd totter and the litter yawed sideways, she never lost her amused little grin, which made us believe we might do this. We were redlining from the first step, burning energy we couldn't get back. I knew that would cost us as we made our way down. It took over an hour of 50-foot pushes to tractor the initial half-mile, our bodies absorbing thought and feeling, condensing them into sweat. We collapsed in a small clearing above some fortified steps, cut into living rock. Waylaid hikers streamed past. One of the Juniors held out a water bottle and I gulped, then offered the bottle to Hope. Reggie beat me to it.

"I've been coming to Yosemite since grade school," Hope said to Reggie, "and you're the first black ranger I've ever seen. Can't imagine what it feels like to be you."

Reggie smiled thinly and said, "It's not so bad as all that."

"You're a lousy liar, Ranger Reggie. This place is as

white as the glacier that made it."

"The Miwoks tell it differently," said Reggie.

An uneasy divide, wide as the valley, had always loomed between Reggie and us. He was so much his own man, maybe race only told half the story. Hope closed the distance in four sentences flat. Reggie was just people to her. They talked a little longer and Reggie laughed, and Reggie never laughed. He glanced at me and thrust his chin toward Hope, as if to say, "Who *is* this woman?"

Good question. I put her around 21, likely a runner with her toned legs and the lug-soled trail runners on her feet. Straight black hair, cut stylishly short, and deep olive skin, like a Persian or a Turk, with eyes just as green as imperial jade. And the delicate tattooed line circling her wrist, with the small red heart in the middle. Back then, the only tattooed females I'd seen were biker chicks and convicts. Hope was the future.

Bama and Chet took a knee next to us and Bama asked Hope how she felt.

"Knee's pretty sore," she said, "and my side hurt at first. But it doesn't anymore."

"Better check," said Chet.

Hope glanced at Bama, who said, "Not to worry, ma'am. Chet here's a medical student."

"Only first year," said Chet.

Ever since high school, Chet spent all ninety days of every summer break climbing in the Valley. Never enough but, at that age, three months feels like a year. He'd return in his mind for the rest of his life.

Chet hiked up Hope's t-shirt and we grimaced at the purple hematoma on her abdomen, just below her ribs. Chet gently pressed his hand against the wound, and said, "Better get her down." Bama motioned his head for Chet and me to follow, above Hope's earshot.

"There's some important machinery under that welt," said Chet. "She's three hours out from her accident, and her vitals check out—"

"We're going," Bama cut in. "Now."

We lurched down the lower steps, taking short breathers to shake the sensation back into our hands, setting Hope on a patch of grass and monkeyflowers flanking the trail. Bama kept asking how she felt. Offering her water, raisins, fruit bars. Hope unclipped her straps, sat up, and asked, "What's your real name, Ranger Bama?"

"Bama's okay," said Bama.

"Stop your worrying," she said, grabbing his arm. "I'll be fine. But I still want to know your name."

I mentioned the time we didn't have, and Hope asked Bama about his name again. Injured people often binged on questions like this. A good connection, talking about anything, can crush a lot of fear. But Hope wasn't scared. She was the stranger you meet on a plane or in the barbershop—or on a rescue—and you stamp the heat in your secrets through private disclosure, much as you douse a campfire before moving on. Then you pray to never meet that stranger again so long as you live.

"My name's Beau Dobbins," Bama finally said. His nametag read Dobbins, but "Beau" was news to us. Even the Chief Ranger called him Bama—as in Alabama, his home state—a slightly pejorative handle he lived with.

"Would that be Beaucifus Dobbins?" she asked. Bama flushed a little. "That's world class," said Hope. "Family name, Ranger Dobbins?"

Bama paused, and said, "So they tell me. We gotta get this party moving. We're racing the clock here, ma'am."

"What's up with you two?" she asked, glancing at Bama and me in turn. "You guys act like you shot each other's dog."

The woman had a genius for bluntly asking awkward questions in a way we felt obliged to answer. It was impossible to ignore someone two feet away.

"He's a climber," said Bama, as if I weren't there. "And climbers only respect their own authority. That's the problem right there."

"Your pants are on fire, Ranger Dobbins," she said.

Bama peeled her fingers off his arm and we both said, "We gotta go."

The trail widened slightly so we could handle the carry with two to a side, one on point and another in back. We hoisted the litter and slashed across the middle switchbacks.

"I think you're a frustrated artist," Hope said to Bama as the litter pitched and rolled. "I'm sorta one myself. You play an instrument or anything?"

Bama mumbled, “A little piano, ma’am. But not very good.”

Another lie. A big one. The previous summer, after the annual climbers-rangers softball game, and halfway through our second keg, we straggled into the backcountry ranger’s cabin, which had an old piano in the corner. Bama sat and banged out a medley of ragtime tunes from Jelly Roll Morton, Fats Waller, and Lucky Roberts. All the classic stuff. *The Billy Bob Thornton of the Park Service* was a redneck who’d been touched.

“Pick it up, hilljacks,” said Bama. “It’s dark in two hours.”

But racing up the trail and the toboggan-from-hell had ruined us. It took Reggie two tries to even stand after our next break. We barely made it 100 yards before our hands went numb and our forearms pumped out, and we had to set Hope down on a flat-topped boulder in the shade. Hikers, spent, staggered by.

“Three minutes,” said Bama. “Not a second more.”

“The climbers and the rangers,” said Hope. “How come you’re working together?”

Enough already with the questions. Couldn’t she see us cruxing here? She grabbed my arm, so I told her — that ambitious climbers needed the whole summer to round into shape and do their projects. But with the seven-day camping limit, the only way around it meant working on the rescue team for burrito wages. Climbers came in handy for technical rescues when they broke out the ropes and the tackle; but rescues were run like military operations, and climbers were never huge on taking orders. A few years later, all the rescue rangers *were* climbers. Good ones, too. But not back then.

"But you get to stay here all summer," she said, sweeping her hand across the valley.

"We make it work," I said. "Barely..."

"So, what's up with you and Bama?" she asked.

"Nothing that matters now," I said. It wasn't getting any lighter outside. But Hope was. The second we set Hope down in the shade we saw her skin blanching. Chet tapped the crook in her arm, checking the vein. She sounded a little dreamy when she answered his questions. Chet didn't pull us aside this time.

"She's bleeding inside," he said.

Bama went off. "You said she was fine an hour ago!"

"Two hours ago," said Reggie. "We're gonna need help."

My head felt heavy and my insides raced. An eerie freeze crept through me.

"Grab a few guys off the trail," said Chet, still bent over Hope, "and rotate them in for the carry."

"Get 'em!" said Bama, who jumped over to try and rally Hope, already slurring her words. Chet grabbed Hope's wrist and checked her pulse.

"We're getting her down," said Bama, stepping close and looking right at me, spit flying off his lips. "You hear me?"

We had a debt to pay, known only to ourselves, and

the fear and panic of adding to it thrust us right into each other's face.

"We gotta get going," I said, only half-aware I was gripping Bama's arm. Everything inside me felt like ice. Reggie's legs were gone, but he somehow backtracked up the trail to try and enlist anyone big and fit enough to help.

We grabbed the litter and wobbled off with five carrying: Bama, Chet, and I, and the two Juniors. We fought like crazy, hell-bent to hang on and keep busting down the trail; but our hands opened after 100 feet, and we half-dropped Hope to the ground. She forced a smile, but couldn't hold it for long. Bama jutted between trying to reassure Hope and swearing at creation. We had a hard, vertical mile to go.

Reggie returned with a half a dozen guys, all strangers to each other. Two grabbed the litter from each side as a big Newfie took the front, and another guy took the back, and the train charged down the switchbacks. Bama shot ahead, calling out obstacles and guiding the carry. I kept swapping out up front with the Newfie. I could only manage three or four minutes at a go but, without something to do, only jogging alongside, my mind kept attaching to events from the past, and the freeze made my bones chatter. I could only warm out of it by grabbing the litter again.

Others joined as we descended: an Italian in soccer shoes, a burly Kenyan diplomat, a pilot from the Indian Air Force, and more random strangers we shagged off the trail, and who spontaneously found a teamwork that thawed me out as Hope and the litter jounced down at speed. Ankles twisted. Shins barked off rocks. Grunting sounded in multiple accents—but quietly—so as not to disturb Hope, all as Bama drove the train for greater speed. Chet kept checking on Hope, who started nodding in and out, and he made us set her down where the stream cut across the trail.

Hope's eyes were open but focused on infinity. Bama grabbed her shoulder and said, "Talk to me, girl." She moved her lips but didn't say anything, just stared straight up and a thousand miles past us. Bama gently shook her again. Hope cocked her head a little to the side, as if she recognized something in outer space. Bama couldn't stand it, and said, "What you looking at?"

She wasn't looking at anything. She was listening—to whirling mist and water rolling down the slabs below the falls. Sounds only she could hear. She closed her eyes and breathed out the words, "It's...OK. OK..."

I pictured Hope following those sounds down the trail, left across the buttress to the streaming foggy slabs below the falls. Her body might last another few hours. But the Lost World, I figured, if it was ever a place at all, was always the last stop.

Chet told Bama to call for the Med Evac. The little valley clinic couldn't handle this. Hope needed to get to a trauma unit. "It's gonna be tight," said Chet, who'd interned that summer in a Calgary ER, in Alberta, where his mom came from. Bama called it in, nearly screaming into his radio, the veins jumping off his neck.

Reggie grabbed him by the shoulders and said, "Ain't nobody quitting here, Bama, so don't go sissy on yourself and lose your shit. We got this."

For a second, Bama trembled like an anxious boy and said, "You think?"

"I *know*, you fucking hillbilly," said Reggie, who'd probably waited years to say those words, and which put the thunder back in Bama. He checked Hope then yelled, "Load her up!"

Eight females emerged from nowhere and strode to the column. Word had trickled up the trail and they'd raced down to help. They were members of USA Volleyball, tall as oaks and fit as antelope. One woman grabbed the front of the litter, another the back, as four setters and spikers took each side and we trundled off, Bama jogging ahead, yelling, "Watch the ledge!" and "Left between the rocks!" Twenty men trailed, ready to spell the ballers, but grateful for the relief as we flowed down widening switchbacks, pausing at the hairpin turns.

Bama blared into his radio, "Where's the goddam chopper?" The Valley was graying over.

Hope hadn't spoken for a whole bunch of switchbacks, and her silence was deafening. The volleyball team swapped out with the trailing column, and Chet checked Hope's pulse for a tenth time. Thin but steady.

"*Where's that fucking chopper*?!"

Deep shadows bled over the southern rim of the valley, streaking down the deepening draws, gulches, and rearing north faces. We charged, the bathroom lights in Camp 4 shining through the gloom as the sound of thumping copter blades ricocheted up the valley. We passed Hope from person to person over a lopsided staircase of railroad ties, racing her past the last switchback to the trailhead and reaching the dirt parking lot and the idling Med Evac right as the sun started setting.

Twenty-five exhausted people bent over the litter and watched Hope's green eyes dim. And she faded, in the way a ballad or a movie ends. The medic strapped a blood pressure cuff onto Hope's limp arm and pumped and pumped. But he couldn't pull a reading. The trauma unit in Fresno was 93 miles away, he said, and he said no more.

They slid Hope into the cargo hold and Bama and I stumbled out onto the loop road—blocked for the rescue—and watched the chopper, and Hope, fade to black. We walked away in different directions. I never saw Bama again.

The Jumbo Jet jounced off some turbulence. I dropped from a dreamless sleep and found myself on a plane. Took a minute for my eyes to pull focus on the small video monitor mounted on the seatback, the flight tracker showing the little yellow line edging out across the Atlantic.

I spotted Hope shuffling down the aisle, holding something in her hand and squinting in the blacked-out cabin. She'd find me eventually, so I stood and waved an arm. She took a well-practiced fall into the aisle seat, flipped open the tray table on the empty middle seat, and plunked down a plate with a key lime pie. Dessert from first class. She handed me a fork—a polished metal one, not the plastic articles they give you in economy. The wine, evidently, had worn off.

"Sorry about getting all heavy on you," she said. "But I'm in a kinda strange place these days, and I keep pulling people into it without trying. My boyfriend told me so, when he left for Colorado."

I told her to forget it and handed her back the fork. I never took food for granted. Back in my climbing bum days, we rarely had the good stuff and, even years later, a full fridge always amazed me. But I couldn't eat. I still felt cold inside, even after napping for an hour. I tossed off the triple-shot can of espresso I had in my carry-on, and my head began to clear.

"What takes you to England?" she asked.

"I'm a writer on a show, and we're shooting in Wales next week."

"Good show? Have I seen it?"

"Hope not," I said. "It's fluff. Bottom-feeder stuff."

Hope shrank back in her chair. "We did a concert last week in Baton Rouge," she said. "I'm a singer, by the way, and before the last set, I race backstage and change into heels and this fuck-me dress. I go back onstage and start belting out..." She paused, and jammed the fork into the pie. "Second we hit the bridge I have this sinking feeling that everyone knows I'm a poser. I can do pop, but I despise it. I'm not too good for it. I never said that. But there's hell to pay when I fake anything."

"You can afford it, anyhow, being all rich and shit."

"The Devil doesn't take cash," she said.

"Sounds like a song right there," I said.

"Know how I got through that set?" she asked. "I saw myself back in that litter, at the end. All fog and liquid space. I let the rocking push the words outta me."

She was edging me back to the Valley, and we both knew it.

"Let's not do this," I said.

"Sorry," she said, grabbing my arm. She wasn't sorry. She was the person who put words to the snakes in our soundproof minds, and to the masochism of living there, alone. But it all went miles beyond Hope. This reckoning caged me like a mob loan I'd refused to pay off, and the vigorish was sucking me dry. I ran my finger over the gossamer tattoo circling her wrist.

"You asked about Bama and me," I said.

She raised a hand and said, "Doesn't make your business mine."

"Does now." My tongue started swimming from the triple shot. I didn't fight it. "Couple weeks before your accident," I said, "Bama gets word the sous-chef at the Yosemite Bar and Grill had gone missing. We both know the guy—a trail runner who'd set a bunch of records for out-and-back runs. He'd jogged out to Cloud's Rest. That's a big granite dome in Tenaya Canyon. When he doesn't show at work that night, Bama grabs me and we go searching next morning."

The plane bounced off some currents again and we nearly lost the pie.

"The trail's pretty good," I said, "but it's seven miles back to Cloud's Rest, and it takes us a couple hours to get there. No sign of the sous-chef, so we follow a watershed up toward the dome. Then some wild animal starts howling. Like it's gutshot or something. But it isn't an animal. It's the sous-chef. He's slumped in a heap at the base of Cloud's Rest. Legs shattered and twisted around. Got open fractures on both arms."

I glossed over how the sous-chef had somehow wriggled into a sitting position, with his back against the rock. He must have climbed the low-angled slab just above him, because the views up there are worth it. But he'd fallen, head-first, bouncing and sliding straight into the ground. Whatever face he had was still up on the slab. Eyes, nose, lips, and cheeks—gone. All his front teeth were knocked out and his skull had been ground through in spots. It seemed impossible any creature could still be alive like that. I only told Hope enough to paint the picture—that the sous-chef was unspeakably fucked up. The rest she'd have to hear. In detail. So would I.

"His chest kept rising and falling," I said, "but he hadn't moved or made a sound—till his limbs started flailing like he's on fire. And that heinous wailing again. I ripped open the first aid kit and Bama grabbed the morphine auto injectors, the kind they use for buddy-aid on the battlefield when somebody gets their legs blown off. Lucky a stick graphic showed us how to use them."

I'd compartmentalized the rest of this into a space so small and dense that light couldn't enter or escape. Now it exploded and I could picture it all lit up, like a film on the seatback monitor. I just narrated what I saw:

Bama pulls off the safety plug, rams the injector against the sous-chef's thigh, thumbs the firing plunger and twenty MGs of morphine race into him. His limbs stop flailing and his shrieks die off. Bama stumbles over to some scrub and throws up. Then the chef is wailing again, and his busted limbs start flapping against the rock. Bama grabs another injector, pulls off the plug and holds it over the sous-chef's thigh. His hand shakes so badly he can barely hold the thing. That'll kill him, *I say.* You know that. *And Bama says,* It better! *Now we're playing God. I don't say anything and Bama yells,* What would you want? *The sous-chef wails again. I reach and cup my hand over Bama's and we fire home a second dose. He flatlines in less than a minute.*

I'd waited so long to put words to this it rushed out of me like a flash flood. It took me a minute to catch back up with myself. The images still played on the monitor, but weren't solid like before and the details kept thinning out, as New York fell behind us on the flight map. I didn't feel so cold anymore. Just hollow.

"We wrapped him in the tarp," I said, "so the animals couldn't get him. Bama radioed in and a team met us on the trail for the carry-out. We got him back to the road head around nine p.m. The doctor at the clinic, who signed the death certificate—he told us no human being could ever survive those injuries. The chief ranger said we'd done the right thing. But we'd done it for the wrong reasons: not to help the chef, but to kill his awful wailing. To make him dead so we could wrap him in the tarp and not have to look at him anymore. That's why Bama and I couldn't look at each other. We made sure we didn't have to—till you went and pitched off the Falls Trail."

We sat there, hurtling through space, saying nothing.

"If I was that chef," Hope finally said, "all I'd have wanted is for you to make it go away. You start in with your reasons, and do nothing, I blame you both forever."

"We did it for you," I said.

"I'd like to meet whoever taught us how to do that," she said.

I told her how the chef's friends hiked his ashes to the north rim and dumped them over Yosemite Falls. I pictured the kitchen crew emptying an urn into the torrent gushing off the lip, a half-remembered force much older yet running straight through the you and me.

"I wanna get back there," said Hope, "but probably not with this knee. Maybe you and Bama can carry me up the trail some summer day. If you know where he's at."

"I heard he's teaching music at some community college in Tuscaloosa," I said. This could have been hearsay, but it made me curious about the music she did like.

"Torch songs," she said. "Me and a piano in a smoky little room."

"You'll never earn a first-class seat from singing 'Cry Me A River.'"

"It's yours if you want it," she said, thrusting her chin toward the front and the six empty rows of first-class seats, where I could compartmentalize myself, solo in the dimness.

Sometimes I heard a wailing. The sound felt monolithic, and blotted out the sun. Now it mingled with wind and mist, as water streamed over the rock. The Lost World was not so much a place as a crossroad for living ghosts. And I wasn't so sure I wanted to leave just yet. A ghost doesn't feel, doesn't bleed. You just float in the mist, neither here nor there.

Hope kept talking, taken by the way things mattered. The wonder in her words, her daring as she leaned in, fetching the whole catastrophe—all these things were beacons of a world beyond the sous-chef.

Hope lowered her seatback all the way and said, "Maybe it's gonna be OK." Then she handed me the fork and gazed at the pie. "You gonna eat that, or what?"

N
NW
NE
W
E
SW
ES
S

“Z”

MS. VERNIER HAD DREADLOCKS and red designer glasses back when nobody did. Her puzzling femininity felt like the pull of the sun, and threw us boys sideways as she floated about the front of the class, dreaming out loud about "Flowers for Algernon" and "Thank You, Ma'am." My eyes kept glancing at the clock hanging on the wall above her. The bell finally rang, and I bolted to the diamond to slug baseballs and chew soggy brown quids of Beech-Nut tobacco, a soul-torquing vice recently acquired thanks to left fielder Randy McDowell, who I'd learned to trick-or-treat, chase girls, smoke, pilfer beer, and skip class with since first grade.

For two hours we'd try like mad to smash line shots over the chain-link fence, where they'd carom off cars in the teacher's parking lot—a feat that was often dreamed about but rarely accomplished; once, by Max Delmonico, only 15 like most of us, but who looked 20 with his size 12 cleats and nascent black moustache. And maybe once a week by Steve Van Noy, broad as a river with thick hairy arms, renowned for his Ruthian drives. Two years later, he got drafted out of high school by the Cincinnati Reds.

We normally beavered away at our fielding and throwing drills, never minding what others were doing since we all had plans to go pro (only Steve did). But when Steve Van Noy took batting practice, everyone stopped and watched his bat rip through the strike zone, the ball exploding off "the lumber" and shrinking to a peanut as it sailed majestically over the fence, once crashing off the principal's Firebird. Van Noy was so much better than the rest of us it was ridiculous. It later made me marvel at how good the major leaguers actually are, since Van Noy, all-everything in high school, never got past Double-A ball, still two rungs short of the bigs.

Practice ended around five p.m. We'd shower, change into street clothes, and plod for home, which averaged a mile or two. We'd lived in the same town, gone to the same schools, had played every sport on every team offered, always together. Yet on the weary march home we'd usually go it alone, shambling along with our thoughts, fixated on one thing: food.

The route home took us north, through a big intersection at Foothill and San Antonio and past a busy shopping center with a Winchell's Doughnut House on the corner, a regular boot camp for diabetes, with its square, white tin crown, floor-to-ceiling windows, and signature neon sign on top. Whenever we had lunch money left over, we'd stumble into Winchell's, pester Haggie, and buy a glazed jelly or maple bar, or whatever remained on the trays. We'd inhale the pastry in three bites, and the swift blast of sugar and grease would push us down the road.

Haggie ran Winchell's and was the only employee we ever saw working the counter. About her nickname: when we were freshman and newcomers to Upland High and Winchell's Donut House, Max Delmonico and I dropped in after school and Haggie snarled at us for no good reason. This confused but thrilled us because we were wise guys who valued anyone with the moxie to push back against our budding aggression. Naturally, we dropped by Winchell's the next afternoon as well, and she snarled at us again.

"She ain't human," said Max as we slogged for home. "She's Hagatha." The name stuck, though we later shortened it to Haggie.

She had raven black hair, prematurely shot with gray and always tied in a gaudy-colored scarf. Her finely drawn features must have been striking way back when (at the time I put her at around 40), but her expression had fossilized into a scowl, as though someone had twisted her arm forever. She wore baggy, long-sleeved baker's whites, and her hands were always dusted with flour. She was waspish towards us, unless we were broke, and she'd grudgingly gift us a doughnut—if we'd clean the place.

By early evening, after practice let out, the dozen tables inside Winchell's were splattered with coffee and strewn with cups and sticky napkins. Haggie, hands on her hips and frowning at the massacre, would grumble, "The pigs!" in her thick, Slavic accent (shortstop Chase Novak swore she hailed from Transylvania). Then she'd thrust a broom into our hands.

Winchell's sold doughnuts, coffee, and pop; no proper food so no dishes, and it only took minutes to tidy things up. Haggie would fork over a doughnut and we'd hit the road. This arrangement only held for the first person to claim it. Everyone else had to pay, something Haggie never budged on. We'd sometimes beg, but her face, latticed with frown lines, refused to soften. She'd jut her chin toward the road and say, "You go now," in her clipped, wonky argot.

I'd sometimes swing by Winchell's on my way to school, just to load up on Haggie's guff. Soon as I pushed through the door she'd glower and say, "You no money." Sometimes I did. Other times I'd spend my lunch money, plunking a few coins onto the counter. She'd go to the back and return with a hot cinnamon roll or a bear claw, dripping with glaze, and say, "You stupid. Go school." I'd give it right back but she'd moved on to other customers, or retreated to the kitchen, as though I didn't exist. She was, as pitcher Greg Martin said, "Hard as a Louisville Slugger."

During our sophomore year at Upland High, our team went fifteen-and-two and we liked our chances going into league finals. Local sports writers felt we had a shot at the state title, till we faced Chino High and future Astros hurler Mark Stein, whose fastball clocked in the mid-90s. Stein blanked us four-to-nothing, and we had to like it. Steve Van Noy hated it. He'd slugged fourteen homers in eighteen games and, by missing out on the state tourney, the pro scouts couldn't watch him launch those titanic drives. The scouts knew all about Steve, and I kept telling him so as we walked home after Stein shut us out. It was already dark and we were famished, so we bee-lined for Winchell's.

We found Haggie tonging the remaining doughnuts into a cardboard carton. An overhead fan stirred the soupy air. Sweat streamed down Haggie's neck in the heat of early June. She even had the sleeves on her baggy white shirt rolled up—a first. She kept loading those doughnuts, grease bleeding out the edges of the carton. She sneered. "You no money."

"I got your money right here," said Steve, who pulled a

wadded dollar bill from his jeans pocket. He had to hoof it to the foothills below the reservoir—three miles, easy—and at his size, plus after going nothing-for-four against Stein, it'd take more than one doughnut to get him there.

"Give us four of them Boston Creams," said Steve. Five or six were still left, sagging through the trays.

"You stupid," said Haggie. "They old."

I glanced at the greying pool, like candle wax, spreading out below the dissolving row of Boston Creams. Made my mouth water.

"Just hand 'em over, will ya?" said Steve.

Haggie stuffed four chocolate-covered bombs into a waxy white bag and barked out, "Dollar," exchanging the bag for Steve's crumpled bill. That's when I saw the tattoo on the outside of Haggie's left forearm—a "Z" followed by several numbers in fading black ink, ragged, and off-center. My juvenile mind couldn't imagine why she would get such a coarse emblem. I pointed at the tattoo and said, "What is that?"

Haggie's eyes darted to her forearm and she yanked down her sleeve and stared at us, or at a forest fire or a plane wreck far in the distance. Haggie dropped the bill onto the counter, walked back into the kitchen, and pulled the door closed behind her. Steve and I slunk outside and silently walked up San Antonio Avenue. We didn't eat the doughnuts.

"Hey," Steve finally said. "She goes and gets a shitty tattoo, it ain't our fault."

"Like a phone number or something," I said. "With a 'Z' to start. See that?"

Steve mumbled, "Yeah," but we hadn't yet seen how there are shadows you cannot outrun. That mutations occur on a cosmic scale which slaughter all purpose and meaning—and burn people to ashes in a flash. The look on Haggie's face. I took it to sleep with me that night.

We lost the next game and nobody cared. The few times I saw Steve, we barely acknowledged each other because Haggie still stood between us, her eyes glassy as cat-eye marbles. The season ended a couple weeks before summer break, and I took another route home so I didn't have to walk past Winchell's Donut House. Once summer ball began, we practiced at Memorial Park, a few miles across town from Upland High. I'd have no reason to visit the campus, or Winchell's, for the rest of the summer.

The day after my 16th birthday and two days after school let out, I started working early shifts at Dewey Jarvis' Chevron, a full-service gas station out on east Foothill Boulevard. My dad was a local family doctor and Dewey, one of Dad's patients. Both men were old-school, believing when a boy could work for pay (at 16 in California), he did. So I pumped gas and changed tires and faced humanity with its mouth open and shirt untucked. The station was a block away from Memorial Park. My shift ended at four p.m. and I'd walk five minutes along Foothill Boulevard right to baseball practice. A pretty sweet arrangement.

The summer heat scorched, the smog suffocated, and

more people streamed into Jarvis Chevron than Liquor Barn. I didn't mind because I was learning the secrets of the world. Everyone needs gas so I witnessed the entire parade—grifters trying to shortchange me, women wearing sunglasses but no pants. I even met jazz bandleader, Stan Kenton, on his way to a gig in Riverside. He drove a silver Porsche Boxer and needed oil. I met a mariachi band in matching chocolate waistcoats with gold piping on the sleeves, who dropped by in a clunker van loaded with drums and those fatty guitars. They had a big basket of tamales and enchiladas, wrapped in tinfoil, that we heated on the engine manifold. Dewey joined in, providing cold sodas from the pop machine, and we had a *banquete* right under the awning, next to the gas pumps. I was joining the larger world all at once, and it felt amazing.

A few times a week Max, Greg, Randy, and others from my team would drop by the station (Steve was in San Diego playing on the Junior Olympic squad) and we'd go on and on about the LA Dodgers, our local pro team. And pitcher Fernando Valenzuela, cult star of "Fernandomania." And the hateful "Matt the Bat" Williams, All-Star third baseman for the rival San Francisco Giants, who even Fernando could never get out. But mostly we talked about our next season at Upland High. Most of us were returning. We were filling out and growing up by the minute, and could all drive now, so the state title, we all agreed, was ours to lose.

Toward the end of summer, with the Dodgers holding a two-and-a-half-game lead over the Giants, a silver-haired man pulled into the station in a sky-blue Cadillac Coupe de

Ville. A regular land yacht. And beautifully polished and maintained. He said "Fill it up" in proper American, but he had a croaky accent that punched the wrong syllables. I carefully cleaned his windshield and rear glass, too. No smears or streaks. I checked his tires, water, and oil—all fine—as the big Caddy took on twenty-two gallons of ethyl. I ran his credit card through the swiper and brought the receipt back on the plastic tray for him to sign. He reached out from the window and I saw the coarse, fading line of small numbers tattooed on his left forearm. I could still picture the annihilating blankness on Haggie's face.

"I knew a woman at a donut shot who had a tattoo like yours," I said. "Except you got a triangle before the numbers. She had a 'Z.' When I asked her about it—" I stopped because the man looked right at me now. "I was... curious, that's all," I said.

The man's face set hard, yet he looked strangely pleased I'd noticed his tattoo and asked about it. He shook out a cigarette from a hard pack, lit it (strictly forbidden in a gas station), blew out a cloud and, speaking what sounded like German, reeled off a string of numbers, which I imagined corresponded to those on his tattoo.

"We all get the numbers when they take us to Auschwitz," he said. "The number becomes my second name. When they wake us in the night, you say your number in the *Deutsch*." He ground out the smoke in the ash tray and started the car. "Some few of us get out and make a life," he said, "but we never forget the number." He patted the tattoo, nodded, and I nodded back. I watched his big blue Cadillac roll out onto Foothill Boulevard and vanish in the distance.

I'd heard about Auschwitz, but the few histories I'd read in school were all broad strokes, largely sanitized, as if the textbook writers were scared or ashamed about the details. I discovered those in an old magazine I fished from the Upland City Library, about World War II concentration camps. Auschwitz in particular. And its sub-camps, Birkenau and Monowitz, with black-and-white photos I wish I'd never seen. And how they assigned inmates with identification numbers tattooed across their left forearms, sometimes including a symbol first: a triangle for Jews, and a "Z" for Romani. So Haggie was a gypsy. Few escaped Auschwitz alive and I'd met two in a matter of months. What were the odds? But I saw everything at Jarvis Chevron. I'd have to go visit Haggie, who I'd thrown back into those death camps with my thoughtless question. I needed a plan.

My youngest sister started school a week before I did and she had played the genie in "Aladdin," wearing a costume that made her look like a mermaid, which they had accessorized with several scarves. I pinched the loudest scarf, a blinding tangerine color, and drove my mom's Impala down San Antonio Avenue toward Winchell's Donut House. I'd read how gypsies roam, but Haggie was still there in her baker's whites, her hair tied in a lavender scarf. She looked at me vacantly while I pulled a dollar bill from my wallet and carefully placed it on the counter, then laid the scarf alongside.

"The money's for a cinnamon roll," I said, "if you got any left."

"In back," she said, as if she'd never set eyes on me.

"The scarf's for you."

She crooked her head. "Where you get?"

"From my sister. She wore it in a play."

Haggie went blank and didn't move—like when a film jams in the projector. Finally, she went back into the kitchen and returned with a cinnamon roll on a napkin set on a paper plate. A caring gesture but, when our eyes met, the world stopped dead from the ineluctable profundity of feelings that flew up out of the earth. Hundreds of thousands of ghosts had chased me into that stifling tin box and would hear nothing about how sorry I was. Maybe a ghost's greatest fear is solitude, and being forgotten; so they hold us hostage till their story is shared and felt, all the way down. The scenes I saw in that magazine were not something I could ever make right or chase away with some lurid costume scarf. So a boy came to know that the long lost—an old man in a blue Cadillac, a greying gypsy in baker's whites—deserve a prayer of silence, because one word spoken is way too much and a thousand is never enough.

Haggie put her hands on the dollar and the scarf and pushed them toward me. I pushed them back. She made change for the dollar but didn't touch the scarf.

"I think you steal scarf," she said. "From sister."

"What if I did?" I said.

She didn't smile, exactly. More of a *Really*? kind of smirk. But the world was turning again, and we both were somehow on it. I grabbed the paper plate and the donut, left the scarf, and turned to go.

Haggie chuckled in her inimitable Romani argot: "You stupid."

CHICKENSHIT SHARK

PHIL AND I SWUNG FACE-DOWN in hammocks, trying to spit through rifts in the floor, when Mrs. Davenport screamed bloody murder from the next room over. A fiddler crab had scampered across her bedspread and fled across the slats, followed by shoes and bottles and whatever she could grab and hurl at the invader.

"*Viva la Mexico*!" Phil laughed.

For months I'd counted the hours till we could escape our little bedroom community in SoCal and spend Easter vacation in Baja, California, with the Davenports: my best friend, Phil, and his folks, Harold "Jefe" Davenport and his wife, Katherine Putnam Davenport, a Jane Eyre knockoff on triple sec and valium. We'd only arrived in Baja that afternoon, but Mrs. Davenport couldn't bear the *casita* another second.

Jefe loaded Mrs. Davenport's three suitcases into the rental Jeep for their evacuation to the Hotel Rosario La Paz, a few miles away. We could come if we wanted to. We didn't. Jefe promised to swing by in the morning to take us out for breakfast. The Jeep wheeled off, leaving Phil and I alone. We were both 16 years old.

The Davenport *casita* lay close by a dirt road, in a copse of bamboo, set on oak pylons and cantilevered over gulf waters renowned for sport fishing. The front of the house had a weathered, wooden front door, white-washed plaster walls and no windows—a façade left plain to limit break-ins. Jefe spent a bundle trimming out the inside, with portraits of Aztec noblemen and a few San Sebastian bullfighters on the reed walls, combed steer hides on the wooden floor, and faux Olmec artifacts staged in cabinets against the den walls. But here in Baja, the electricity was on and off (mostly off), the humidity killed cockroaches, and the flooring was so warped we could watch the anxious ocean through the gaps. A chrome-plated horseshoe hung over the kitchen door for *suerte*, or luck. Now we had the run of the place. Phil rifled the liquor cabinet and came away with a black earthenware jug, sealed with a waxed cork.

"The real *mierda*," said Phil.

He drew out the cork with his teeth and swilled two fingers of tequila. A spasm rattled through him but his smile didn't break when he handed me the bottle. We'd watched *Fistful of Dollars* and *The Good, The Bad and the Ugly* ten times each, and admired how Clint Eastwood tossed off 100-proof hooch like branch water. So we drank our liquor with impunity. We moved to the back where a plank staircase descended between two rotting pylons, from the den straight into the sea.

At the bottom step, tied off to a pylon, bobbed a frail and leaky dinghy. We sat on the last step with our legs in saltwater and gazed out over the moon-rinsed gulf, talking about climbing at Tahquitz, and maybe doing some bullfighting here in La Paz, if they'd let us. We tilted the bottle and I could feel the tequila in the roots of my hair like electricity, and it arced straight into my toes.

Phil spotted the giant cutlass carving through the water, flashing as it swiveled in the moonlight.

"Shark," Phil whispered.

I climbed a couple stairs as Phil jumped into the dinghy, snatched an oar and madly bashed the water.

"Frenzied movements attract them," said Phil. "I read so in *Argosy*."

"Man, that fin's big as I am," I said, clinging to a pylon. "Sure you wanna be fuckin' with it?"

Phil thrashed the water harder still. I moved to the top step as the fin swept close by the dinghy, circled under the house and plowed back into the deep. Phil jumped from the dinghy, splashed up the stairs, and into the house. He charged back down the stairs with the remains of our chicken dinner and chummed the water with bones and gizzards. Several times, the gleaming fin cruised past, but never as close as the first time.

"Blood," Phil said. "We need blood." And he hurled the tequila bottle into the sea. The moon arced over the gulf and our eyes stayed glued on the wrinkled sea till we straggled back into the house after midnight. Dawn came round before I drifted off in my hammock, picturing a great fin circling under the bedroom floor.

I woke late the next morning and found Phil studying the chrome horseshoe hanging above the kitchen door. Mr. Davenport had already come and gone, and Phil showed me a fat wad of *peso* notes to prove it. His mother had a fever and Jefe couldn't leave her alone in the hotel. We'd have to fetch our own breakfast. Phil reached above the doorjamb and yanked the horseshoe off the wall.

"We're going fishing, amigo."

We jogged over to the paved road, swung onto an autobus, and jumped off in central La Paz, grabbing a shrimp cocktail in one stall, ogling the *señoritas* in others. We found an old man hunched over a foot-powered grinder, and he milled one end of the silver horseshoe into a pick. *Peso* notes furiously changed hands, Phil rattling off *Español* like a local. Mrs. Davenport lived at their family estate in La Jolla. But Phil grew up around Jefe, a kook gentleman anthropologist who'd fooled away nearly thirty years annoying natives and studying ancient cultures deep in the Peruvian rain forest. So Phil could speak Spanish like Cantinflas.

We hustled on through the fish market, ankle deep in mullet offal. At another stall, a fleshy woman, her cavernous cleavage dusted with talc, cut chain off a gigantic, rusty spool.

"For leader," said Phil, grabbing my arm and racing off.

Phil bought 100 meters of polypropylene rope from another lady in a booth hung with black velvet murals of *Jesucristo*. Meanwhile, her husband welded the chain leader onto the sharpened horseshoe, sparks from his torch raining over the Messiah like shooting stars.

"Now for the bait."

We took a cab to the slaughterhouse, across the street from the cemetery. An autobus took us back to the *casita,* me laden with a giant bull's heart wrapped in brown paper and a plastic bucket of bloody slop so heavy it put my hand to sleep. On the stairs behind the house, Phil baited the sharpened horseshoe with the ruby bull's heart, duct taped a soccer ball to the chain leader a foot below where he'd tied on the rope, coiled the line on the stairs, and lashed the free end around a creaky pylon. Then he hefted the bucket of entrails into the dinghy.

"You either watch the line here in the bow, or row. Your choice."

"I thought we were going to just chuck the thing in from here."

"Shark won't go for it. You saw how he shied away last night. And anyway, I bought all this rope."

100 meters of nylon rope seemed a piss-poor reason to row into shark-infested waters in a leaky dinghy full of blood and guts, but Phil had already jumped in the boat, yelling, "Come on, *hombre*," in his best Clint Eastwood voice. "It's a two-minute job."

I took the oars and rowed straight out into the gulf, little geysers spewing through cracks in the overloaded dinghy. The house slowly receded, the line slithering out from its coil. The water rose over my sneakers. Fifty yards out, Phil tossed the bucket overboard and a red halo bled out around us.

"That sucker's any closer than Acapulco, he'll smell this," said Phil. "Believe it."

"I do."

Phil hurled the big heart overboard with a plunk, the weight yanking out the chain leader, which chattered over the dinghy's low gunwale. The soccer ball shot out and sank. Phil panned the ocean for a moment; the ball popped up a few feet away; the waters churned, and he screamed, "Pull, man, pull!"

I heaved at the oars, my heart thundering in my ears, the dinghy nearly hydroplaning. Phil kept bailing with a coffee can, yelling, "Put your back into it or we're goners!"

I rowed harder and faster, trying to retrace the line floating on the water, marking the way back home. The flimsy oars nearly bent in half as Phil screamed to go faster and faster till my oars drove like bee's wings. Twenty yards from the house, we both screamed, breathless and terrified, the dinghy shin-deep and sinking by the second. A final heave and I powered right into the stairs and we stampeded over each other and through the house and out the front door, finally collapsing at the feet of a man selling shaved ice from a pushcart. Phil lay in the dirt, sucking air.

"Not that we're afraid to die or anything," Phil laughed.

After a few minutes, we stole back into the house, tiptoed through the hall, through the narrow den, past the glassware and artifacts, pausing at the open door and the stairs below and staring out over the gulf at the line sleeping on the surface and the soccer ball bobbing peacefully 50 yards away. There wasn't so much as a mackerel on the line. Never had been.

"Chickenshit shark," Phil mumbled.

For several hours we sat hip to hip on the stairs, staring out at the bobbing ball so hard the flat horizon and the heat mirages of high noon put us in a trance. Everything went quiet.

"Wonder where the gulls went?" I asked.

The rope jumped from the water, the staircase groaned, and splinters flew off the pylon as the line lashed itself taut as a bowstring.

"He's hooked!" cried Phil.

We lunged for the rope as the pylon bowed against the stairs. Rusty nails sprang from fractured planks and sand crabs scurried from dark places. Far out on the rolling blue plane carved an invincible fin, a roil of water and a jagged snap. A scythe-shaped tail curled on itself and the rope went slack against the pylon. A gathering surge tore straight toward us like a submarine approaching the surface. The fin swerved maybe 10 yards off and headed out to open sea, fast as a cigarette boat.

"Grab the rope, or the house is going with him," Phil yelled, lunging for the line.

No chance to check the monster, but I grabbed the rope because Phil said to. The shark hit the slack line, wrenching me off the stairs and straight into carnivorous waters. I crabbed from the water and over the stairs and didn't stop running till the den, where I stood, breathless, witless, and shitless, seawater pouring onto the rug. My trunks had nearly dried before I crept back out to the stairs. The line went slack, then taut. Then slack again. We pulled like mad.

"*Eres tan* ugly *que hiciste llorar a una onion*, you *pinche* cocksucker!" Phil yelled.

The rope smoked through my hands. We pulled some

more and Phil kept swearing, calling up the remotest, most colossal vulgarities, so piquant in his Spanglish I could only pull in awe. It was genius.

After an hour, we'd gained a little. With the rope doubled around a pylon, we had enough purchase to lock the beast off, even spool in some little rope when the tension eased for a second. Several times it broke the surface, obsidian eyes glinting in the sun. The monster would relax for a moment and we'd win a little rope, the line would twang tight, the pylon would creak and the stairs would twist and shudder under our feet. The line seared through my hands and the saltwater stung like hell.

The line went lax for several minutes and Phil said, "Jefe got this place from Old Man Daley, or from the widow Daley." He spit into his palms, rubbed his hands together and reclasped the rope, ready for the next strike. "Old Man Daley used to visit on weekends from San Diego, drink some, and fish for tiger sharks," he went on. "One Sunday, he didn't return home, so a brother or cousin came down looking. 'Cept all he found, on a sandbar under the house, was a leg bone and a *huarache*."

Phil often enriched the story because he couldn't hack it whenever the line went slack, even for a minute.

"This ain't working," said Phil, staring out to sea. "Lock that *monstruo* off for a sec." He stomped up the stairs and shot into the *casita*.

I braced against the pylon and held fast as the house filled with whoever Phil could snag off the dirt road: dark-haired boys, street urchins, even the man with the pushcart. Phil returned to the steps, unwound the rope from the pylon, ran the line from the water over the stairs and through the den, down the hall, and right out the front door.

The gang turned its back on the *casita,* each man and boy clasping the rope over their shoulder, Phil yelling, "*Hale, hale, caballeros*!" The tug-of-war was on.

Phil joined me once more on the crumbling stairs, hauling hand over hand. Out in the gulf, a huge swell spooled toward us as the shark, big as a four-man bobsled, bee-lined for the *casita*.

"Let off," I yelled, releasing the rope and backpedaling away, "Tell them to let the fuck off!"

But the gathering crowd had forged out past the road, thirty feet churning the dust. Phil and I jumped to a pylon when, with one titanic lurch, they hauled the opalescent monster to light. It flopped lengthwise onto the buckling stairs, the silver horseshoe hooked deep through its saw-toothed lower jaw, the line taut as a guy-wire.

The shark lurched, its bear trap maw snapping. The crowd yanked the beast right past us and over the stairs, its sandpaper flank rasping the skin off my arm as it jackknifed through the open back door and into the den. With a snap of its jaws, it clipped the legs off the rosewood table.

"Let off, for Christ's sake," I screamed from the stairs, "Let it go!"

But every able person along the dirt road had clasped the

rope, all hauling for pride, country, and the hell of it. But half a ton of shark wasn't going easy. A smashing tail and the cabinet was gone, the Olmec artifacts splintered into shards, the Spanish glassware crushed to sand. Colossal teeth shredded filigreed wood, ripped the hides off wicker chairs. A flip and a twirl, and it unraveled the Malaga rug.

The heaving crowd dragged the monster farther through the narrow den. Purple blood splattered white partitions. A deepwater kip, an airborne nose butt, and a wall caved in. Salt-rotted wood fractured and floor slats snapped to attention as the ceiling dropped a yard and parted to show a splintered smile of Mexican sky.

"Sweet Baby Jesus!" Phil screamed. "*HALLLLLLLLLE!*"

And how the mob pulled. The great monster died ten times, and erupted back to life, knocking plaster off the hallway walls, murdering the grandfather clock, blasting the front door off its hinges.

At last the noble creature lay outside, its hornblende eyes locked on infinity, its jagged mouth open. A *vato* with a ball cap probed the cavity with a tree branch and, in a final show of sea force, the huge mouth snapped shut. The *vato* jumped back with a wooden stub in his hands, yelling, "*¡Qué bárrrrrrbaro!*"

We all stood 'round in a daze, staring at the great sea

monster as kids prodded it with branches and rakes. A handful of girls and women, either walking or driving past, had also joined in on the haul, and co-ed groups took turns posing for pictures taken with an old Kodak Brownie Phil swore had no film in it. Word of the conquest spread down the dirt road. Several *Federales* turned up, followed by a flatbed truck from the fish market. It took ten of us to logroll the creature onto the lift and into the bed of the truck. In five more minutes, the shark existed only in memory. The crowd wandered off and, once again, Phil and I were alone.

I was grated raw, rope-burned, sunburned, splintered, and bloodied, one sneaker gone, my hands two pulpy knobs. Phil barely had a mark, but the *casita* was trashed.

We tried a dozen different lies on each other but couldn't build an excuse as big as that shark or the wreckage it caused. Phil went to the Hotel Hidalgo to try to explain and, in an example of his transcendental luck, he found his parents packing to leave on the next plane for the States. His mother thought another night in Mexico might kill her. Without reservations, they could secure only two seats on the afternoon Air Mexicana flight to Los Angeles. But Jefe had booked us on a later flight that night. The Davenports would wait for us at the Captain's Club in the LA airport, and next day we'd all go to Disneyland.

We raced back to the *casita* and, after wandering through the ruin for several minutes, Phil said, "Shark left us no choice here...but to torch it."

"Torch what?"

"The *casita*. We burn the place down."

I pictured myself in a Mexican jail. Forever.

"You want to try and explain this?" Phil laughed, glancing at the ocean through a ten-foot hole in the floor, then up through the rent in the roof.

"The *casita*'s dusted. *Acabó*."

"How do we explain the fire?" I asked.

"We don't," Phil smiled. "That's the glory of it. It burns down after we're gone. And it will."

Phil ran into town and returned with a big can of kerosene and two votive candles. We threw our suitcases into the cab waiting on the dirt road. Phil soaked the demolished den with kerosene, planted two candles on the buckled floor, lit them, walked out the open door, and got into the cab.

As we ground off the tarmac, we spotted smoke out east, a thin plume rising off the fringe of the sea. Phil leaned back in his seat and said, "Wonder how much that sucker weighed?"

When Jefe returned to Mexico, he found two shrimp boats tied to the blackened pylons where the *casita* once stood. Nobody knew how the fire had started, or when.

A decade later, shortly after his 26th birthday, Phil and his two kayaking partners paddled into an unexplored river in Sumatra and no one ever saw them again. Phil already had a name, and the press, though respectful, said anyone living so over-the-top was bound to fall sooner than later. They didn't understand Phil was not built for the slow burn. That's not an excuse. From the day I first met Phil at Pioneer Junior High School, the intimacy of risk had hooked him as deeply as the horseshoe hooked that shark. Mexicans have a term—"*el gran varón*"—for major dudes like Phil: a hypothesis made of impossibilities, none of them built to last.

GREAT WAVE

DUKE KAHANAMOKU WAS AN OLYMPIC swimming champion and a legendary surfer who Sal and I learned about during junior high. Our homeroom teacher surfed, like us, and he had a Xerox copy of the *Surfer* magazine with Duke's last interview, with pictures of the Hawaiian with the gold medal standing next to his 15-foot koa wood longboard. And another shot of the champion as an old man, walking in the sand out by Diamond Head. Sal xeroxed the xeroxed copy and, in a few weeks, we could recite the good parts word for word, especially the bit about the famous wave at Waikiki, which the Duke rode for over a mile before kicking out. "A ride for the ages."

Duke talked about another great wave he knew was waiting for him, and how someday he would catch it.

"But this time I'm not kicking out," he said. "I'll just keep on going." This part didn't sound exciting, so we only read it once.

The Duke was 77 years old when he did his interview, and Sal was 19 when doctors told him he had a month to live. By then, I'd traversed into rock climbing and hardly surfed anymore; but it killed me to watch my friend shrivel away, and I didn't have a clue. Right at the end, I dug out the old xeroxed copy of *Surfer* and I read the interview to Sal one last time. I went over the last bit twice, the part we always skipped before.

By then, Sal couldn't talk, but he clearly could hear what I said and he never struggled again. His girlfriend wondered why. She didn't know the Duke had been our first hero, and all along he'd waited for that great wave—

and for Sal, because the Duke didn't like to surf alone. Now he wouldn't have to. He reached back and pulled Sal onto a perfect blue curl on a perfect blue day. And they didn't kick out, either. Not this time. They just kept on going.

N
NW
NE
W
E
SW
ES
S

THE RABBI

MOST OF MY CLASSES were killing me, so I welcomed the rare fluff course offering full credit. Everyone else did, too, so my junior year came around before I got a chair in The Rabbi's *Birding in the Greater Pomona Valley,* the alluvial basin formed by the Santa Ana River and its tributaries, and home to my little college.

Mort Novak was no rabbi, but we all called him that because he often wore a yarmulke and looked hard into things. During our first day in class, someone asked about the textbook and The Rabbi read a passage by T.S. Eliot, warning never to read commentary about a poem till you read the poem itself, neat, like sight-reading sheet music. This was The Rabbi's third time teaching the birdwatching course and, the way things had gone, students didn't observe birds so much as they thumbed through the birding guide. Eliot wouldn't like that, and The Rabbi hated it. So this class would learn ornithology through direct observation. "And we'll write our own book," said The Rabbi. Here was a man working out a problem. Now we were part of it.

Each of us fifteen students were issued high-powered binoculars, and we followed The Rabbi out to the leafy courtyard in the Humanities Center and started scanning the big sycamore trees for birds. Only when I had a woodpecker in the crosshairs did I realize I'd never truly watched a bird, except for crows on powerlines or toucans in the zoo. Birds were everywhere in Southern California, or anywhere there's water (there are currently around fifty birds per person on earth). But I noticed them only in passing, and never in such handsome detail. Still, the book proposal felt unlikely. The class included science geeks, wannabe novelists, and fussy, brainiac coeds who could recite *The Bell Jar* from memory—hardly the squad to beat the bush searching for vultures.

"You'll need to keep notes," said The Rabbi, as he handed out Champion Wiremaster 100-sheet notebooks (I still have mine). "And keep the binos with you." That was it.

Students squirmed. Barely an hour into birding and the course and The Rabbi were feeling monolithic. Who didn't check expert sources when sussing out anything, one egghead wanted to know.

The Rabbi didn't care. Whatever Darwin did down in the Galápagos, do that.

The unknown is daunting. Even if it's just watching birds in the sky whose Latin names I never learned and couldn't pronounce anyhow. How am I sure what I'm looking at? What if my descriptions are all wrong? The plus side is, as a total ignoramus, I enjoyed a near-vertical learning curve, so long as I paid attention.

Walking across campus, I found myself noticing the ubiquitous sound of birds, stopping to glass a robin or a jay. I lived in the dorms, in an upstairs room the size of a bathroom on JetBlue, made bearable by throwing open the window. This looked out at a big Fremont cottonwood, where birds of many feathers gathered as I skimmed excruciating passages from Mary Barton. Who kept piping that melody? That two-note screech? That funky warbling? Background sounds, long ignored, clarified once

I matched a refrain to a particular bird. So it all began. My Wiremaster started filling out.

Of course, comparing notes with other students was a shitshow without some reference point. The few birds we could recognize by name were doves, sparrows, crows, woodpeckers, and hawks, which arrived in such variety we couldn't be sure if Sheila's description fit the same bird Josh ran down in his Wiremaster. The Rabbi took note, and dragooned the photographer for the school newspaper, also a student in our class, and he spent several days photographing birds roosting in the sycamores nearby. And beyond. The Rabbi's classroom soon resembled the aviary wing of the Audubon Society, with 8x10 photos of birds covering the walls. The course immediately caught fire once we could match notes in our Wiremasters with photos on the wall.

Those birds needed names, and The Rabbi said to fashion our own, so we did: Orange Dinky (House Finch); Cue Ball (California Towhee); Caucasian Sandpiper (Snowy Egret); Sky Jacket (Scrub Jay); Candy Ass (Yellow-Rumped Warbler); Piebald (Black Phoebe); Siren (Song Sparrow), et al. To get anywhere with our book project, we couldn't all be watching the same species, said The Rabbi. We had to pick one bird to follow and document. I went with the Windjammer (Red Tailed Hawk). I'd spotted one on our first field trip to nearby Puddingstone Reservoir. So did LeRoy, from Compton, California, who looked a little like Djimon Hounsou but could crunch numbers with Euclid. At The Rabbi's suggestion, LeRoy and I teamed up to chase down some hawks. Other students joined forces, searching for Cue Balls and Sky Jackets. The Rabbi provided no information beyond where a party might find a given bird. Flight patterns, eating habits, family life—this and whatever else we found supplied the meat and feathers of our future book.

After several months of information gathering, The Rabbi handed out several birding textbooks and we compared the data, much of which we already knew by heart, having learned it firsthand—an impractical method, The Rabbi admitted, for anyone on a schedule. Point was, when we encountered something without labels or names, the experience sparkled with newness. This was the idea when Dumas said to go to Paris and get lost, that you'd never forget it that way.

Thirty-five years after my semester with The Rabbi (who, sadly, the stork reclaimed via COVID-19), I still scan the sky and the treetops for Sky Jackets and Orange Dinkies. When I see one, it's a beautiful thing.

N
NW
NE
W
E
SW
ES
S

THE RIDE

WE PULLED INTO DEL RIO at high noon, mummified by dry heat till another Talon fighter jet streaked in from nearby Laughlin Air Force Base and startled us back to life. We came for the annual George Paul Memorial Bull Riding challenge—"The Toughest Rough Stock Event in Tarnation," according to promotional flyers tacked around the Texas border town. The promo fliers, now collector's items, were Lone Star reboots of the *Return of Godzilla* movie poster—from the 1984 *Kaiju* ("strange beast") movie—where the scaly monster claws the air, swarming with Japanese fighter planes. The Del Rio edition had swapped out the monster for a fire-breathing Brahma bull, with supersonic talons jetting between its horns.

Many champions, past and present, had traveled to Del Rio, including the current points leader out of Henrietta, a five-time world all-around champ and the only bronc on the circuit to ride each rough stock event: bareback, saddle broncs, and bulls. But we'd come to shoot Jaime "Legs" Maldonado for Telemundo, a Spanish language TV channel I occasionally worked for in the late 1980s.

As the writer on a proposed documentary on Legs (which never came off), I had zero qualifications, having never seen a rodeo. My grade-school friend, director Ruben Amaro, filled me in about Legs, Del Rio, and bull riding during the flight from Los Angeles. Brazilian riders were climbing the world standings, said Ruben, worried the sport was getting outsourced. Diversifying, for sure; but most of this crowd looked "rawhide" (American) all the way, from the big Stetson "El Presidente" Cowboy hats on their heads, to the warty, hand-tooled, ostrich skin boots on their feet.

A dozen busloads of fans had spent the day just over the border, in Ciudad Acuña, and many had a load on when the stadium lights clicked on, heat waves rippling over the bleachers. A water truck rolled through the arena, dampening the dusty sod, and made a second pass with one hose turned on the stands, where men stood bare-chested with brown reservoir water washing over them and into their open mouths and blowing the hats off their heads. The announcer, who went by the stage name of Ferris Irons, shuffled around the arena with a wireless microphone, and over a John Philip Sousa march blaring from the PA, in a drawl thick as linseed oil, gave a speech about "these great U-nited States."

Miss Del Rio—a moon-tanned Nefertiti in a string bikini—cantered into the arena on a haughty palomino and half the crowd leaped up whistling and punching the air. As Miss Del Rio circled, cargo bounding and clutching a wooden flag pole as 'Ole Glory rippled overhead, the national anthem sounded over the PA and everybody removed their hats, held them over their hearts, and sang. Ferris Irons eased us into prayer and everyone bowed their heads as he sanctified the riders, the stock, the fans, Yankee Doodle, Old Mexico, and all of creation.

I glanced behind the corrals at the cowboys limbering up and rosining their gear. Each took a knee, pulled off their hats, and closed their eyes. Their faces set like Rodin's *Thinker* as Irons, with the solemnity of last rites, bargained with Lord Jesus Christ about "being on the square" with the cowboys, and "protecting Our Father's champions," and a bunch of other blasphemies in this high kitsch theater.

Irons said, "Ahhh-Mennn," heavy-metal rock burst over the PA, and the crowd exploded.

Telemundo threw little money at these one-off shows, so we didn't have a remote video truck with real-time displays, meaning the two cameramen were shooting "iso"—in isolation. Since we didn't have an on-camera host, once he positioned the cameras to his liking, there wasn't much for Ruben to direct till the interviews after the show. We climbed onto the catwalk above the chute, perched over the last partition and peered down at the first cowboy, straddling the steel fence poles beside the first bull.

The stall could scarcely contain the colossal, slobbering Brahma bull, which snorted and rocked as the cowboy shimmied around on its bare back, trying to find the sweet spot. The bull hated being mounted and clearly considered it as an act of domination, made worse by several men cinching a braided rope around its torso, behind the bulbous hump on its neck. On top of this rope was a thong handle the cowboy clutched with a gloved hand, gummy with rosin. He wrapped the tail of the rope around his "business" hand and yanked it tight enough to pop his knuckles. Meanwhile three other cowboys pulled a second "bucking rope" around the bull's belly, close to its furry, pendulous balls, yanking the line so tight the bull started jumping and jackhammering the stall with its rear hooves, its horned head rearing back fixing to gore the rider on its back, savage eyes red as the sun.

"Coming out with Travis Pettibone on Skoal Psycho!"

The guy working the PA cranked the rock track. Travis Pettibone shoved down his hat, gritted his teeth, and nodded. The gate flew open and a ferocious chunk of snorting, bucking, chuck-roast-from-hell exploded from the chute. It spun left, kicking its back legs so high it nearly did a handstand, snapping its giant head straight back. This was no farm animal, but a highly tuned athlete in its own right. Travis was all flying limbs, yet hung on somehow and the crowd went off.

Skoal Psycho spun right and yawed into the fence, slamming Travis into a sheet-metal sign for Santiago's Steakhouse. The bull whirred away and Travis dropped limp to the ground. The bullfighters' faces were painted like clowns but their job was no joke. One raced up and lured Skoal Psycho toward a guy on a tall black horse, who hazed it to a gate opening to the back corral. The bull shot through the breach knowing another guy was waiting back there to ease the rope slip-knotted around its belly.

The second the arena cleared, paramedics raced in with a gurney. An ambulance with its tailgate open backed to the rear of the arena and they lifted Travis onto the gurney. He sat up and tried to get off, but a bullfighter gently pushed him back down. They loaded Travis up, the ambulance sped off, and another, lights flashing, backed into its place.

I ran back along the narrow catwalk toward the chute, my sneakers sloshing through pools of inky "tabacca" juice crooked old rodeo hands kept spewing onto the slats. Jimi

Hendrix's "Astroman" blared over the PA and Irons yelled, "And it's Cody Lambert on Cajun Moon!"

The gate flew open, Cajun Moon rumbled out and jumped completely off the ground, sunfishing—kicking all fours, twisting and rolling—landing like a runaway train. The bull dug in its hooves, snapped its haunches almost vertical and Cody Lambert shot off into the night, landing in a welter of elbows, knees and trampled soot. He must have wrenched something, but he crabbed to his feet, sprinted to the fence, and clawed up it as the big black Brahma bull rumbled after. Cody looked safe enough, clinging 15 feet up the chain-link, but Cajun Moon kept snorting and bucking beneath him, trying to loosen the rope throttling its gut. The bullfighters decoyed Cajun Moon around and the man on the black horse drove it back into the corral.

The bullfighters were, if anything, more athletic than the riders. One wore football pads and the other a knee brace and soccer cleats. Each time a cowboy ate dirt, and they did most every ride, the bullfighters jumped straight between the bull and the rider, diverting the beast from close range, circling and sidestepping with their bare hands palming off the Brahma's horned head. They occasionally got grazed or kicked and, when Cooter Bodine took a dive on the fourth bull out, the rearing bull's head got under one bullfighter and launched him through the air. That any bullfighter survived an entire rodeo felt like an act of God, and the riders showed their gratitude after every ride with back slaps and fist bumps.

"And give a big Del Rio welcome to D.J. Mulroon on

Black Ratchet!"

The star of this match was not Mulroon—still futzing with his rope—but the bull, whose name brought cheers from the crowd and whose career Irons described with corny flair, ending with his buck-off rate: 96 percent over the last three years. Outside the stadium, several vendors sold t-shirts with silkscreen images of bulls, including Black Ratchet. The bulls were the cowboys' dance partners for the night, said Ruben.

Black Ratchet vaulted out and hobby-horsed wildly in front of the gate, went airborne and "broke in two," uncoupling in the middle, hooves kicking, slammed to earth, and spun like a cyclone. But D.J. hung on for four, five seconds, and the crowd went off again. Black Ratchet juked to one side and D.J. skidded off-center and slipped forward. The bull's rearing head slammed into D.J.'s chest and bashed him back to meet the monster's rearing flank, which drove him into the ground like a railroad spike—a hell of a one-two punch. The bullfighters raced up and drew the bull away, but D.J. Mulroon, bleeding from his mouth and one ear, didn't move. The cowboy lying in the dirt, limbs splayed and dead limp, reminded me of a body piled at the base of a cliff after a climbing or BASE jumping wreck.

"Guy's dead," I mumbled to Ruben.

"*No se*," said Ruben, who broke into Spanish whenever he got excited. "These guys are *duro*, amigo. Give him a chance to get his wind back."

The paramedics jogged in as Irons likened bull riders to

gladiators, slipping in Disraeli's words about courage being fire and Jeremiah's promise the Lord would restoreth. After a few minutes, D.J. came to. The paramedics fitted D.J. with a cervical collar and loaded him onto the gurney. D.J. waved a wilting hand to restless applause. They wheeled him off and into the ambulance, which roared away as another backed into the hot spot.

In the next fifteen minutes I saw two more cowboys body-slammed to the ground and another pitched into the fence and knocked cold. I saw a Brazilian cowboy from Dos Santos get kicked in the groin and another fracture his arm after an electrifying cartwheel exit off a bull called Hum Dinger, which got a standing ovation from the crowd as it rumbled around the arena. Two other riders—the Fawcett brothers, who both looked about 19—went one after the other. Both got rudely chucked off but not hurt. They gathered their gear and stumbled to the dirt lot behind the arena. I traversed the catwalk and watched them slump into a rusty old pickup and sputter off.

Only top riders could afford to fly to rodeos, said Ruben, which, during the season, averaged several a week in cities often thousands of miles apart. The top thirty-or-so guys made their money from sponsorship deals, mostly with beer, chewing tobacco, and apparel companies. Champion-caliber riders often owned planes and might hit two rodeos in the same day, picking and choosing high-profile contests with full purses. But most riders lived closer to the bone, forming partnerships with other wannabe pros who followed the circuit in old pickups like the Fawcetts'. Win or lose, it was right back into the truck for another all-nighter to another rodeo in Tuscaloosa or Dodge or Tuba City. It was a tough go, but they weren't asking for pity and they wouldn't get any.

Buddy Dollarhide, from Checotah, Oklahoma, was the fifteenth rider out and, like most others, went at about five-foot-eight, was lariat thin, and wound tighter than a hair in a biscuit. We watched him swagger to the gate, a bantam rooster in calfskin chaps. He was only the fourth to ride eight seconds to the horn, but he couldn't get off clean, and landed with his legs crossed, flopped on his side and one of the bull's hooves mashed his left ankle. The clowns got the bull's attention and Buddy Dollarhide hobbled off, the jagged white bone jutting through a hole in his boot.

They'd run out of ambulances, so Buddy slouched back on the stairs below the judge's booth off to our left, yelling, "Goddammit! Goddammit to hell!"

A couple other cowboys rubbed his shoulders, and a man with a face like a saddlebag pulled a half-pint of Crown Royal from his hip, twisted off the top and handed it to Buddy. He gulped, hauled up his pant leg, and poured the rest into the top of his boot, screaming, "Son of a fucking bitch!" as the amber liquor streamed out pink through the hole in his boot and over the jutting bone. Buddy chucked the empty bottle and another ambulance wheeled up and took him away.

From the moment Skoal Psycho first burst from the gate a tsunami of adrenaline kept flushing me outside my body. I'd spent a dozen years risking the farm in adventure sports but here, when things went south, a malevolent, two-thousand-pound antagonist wanted to stomp your brains out, which felt like a whole 'nother square dance. How did they ever make this legal, like at any moment the Marines would march in and arrest us for crimes against livestock and humanity.

"Coming out with Waco's own Bobby Reeves on A-Bomb!"

I watched several cowboys limbering up on deck. One glanced back and straight through me, eyes fixed on the oldest drama on earth: man-against-beast. Jumping onto that beast's back was a direct deed hotter than Godzilla's fire, a fictional bugaboo made frivolous by mounting a heap of critical whoop ass, prefaced by hayseed salvation and jingoism, and enacted to a rabid crowd and a feckless few thousand surfing late night cable TV. Raunchy? You bet your ass. Lowbrow? Lower than a feeding trough. But when a bull and a cowboy thundered from the gate, it was real and it was thrilling and strangely transcendent, and the effect was like hauling a magic lantern into the cavern of our lives.

After about three turns, A-Bomb chucked off Bobby Reeves and a clown helped him stumble away to "shake off the bad." Reeves sank to one knee and pawed at his back.

"Getting a few *golpes* is part of the fun for these guys," said Ruben, but this went beyond fun by a country mile.

Ruben clasped the railing, peered over and said, "*Mira,* John. Here's our *paisano.*"

We shuffled over till we were directly above the gate

and had a straight shot of Legs easing onto a big tawny bull. Legs, thick-necked and ripped, couldn't have been taller than five-foot-six. A couple boys yanked on the rope running across the palm of Legs' gloved hand till he muttered, "Yup" in that edging-into-Cajun twang you hear around Stevensville. Legs fiddled with the lash around his hand, folded his fingers, and thumped them with his fist for purchase.

"Boy's got sand," said Ruben, referring to the self-contained grit cowboys so prize.

Back then, Legs was one of the few Mexican-Americans on the pro rodeo circuit. Whenever a rodeo hit Texas, Arizona, or New Mexico, or wherever there were other Mexicans, many turned out to watch Legs ride. Only 24, Legs labored to milk high scores from pedestrian bulls. But on rank stock, where even the best hoped only to stay on board for eight seconds (a qualified ride) and to escape without bleeding, Legs shone.

Legs slid forward so his rope hand was right at his crotch; he nodded quickly, and was gone. When the horn sounded, Legs reached down, loosened the lash, and let the bull's bucking action catapult him off. He landed on his feet in a dead sprint—a nimble, trademark move that earned Legs his handle.

Legs rode differently than the others. He was a little stronger, a little more confident, had a little better balance. When the tawny bull jumped straight up, twisting and rolling, he kicked Legs' center of gravity across the arena. Legs snatched it back with his free hand, cutting the air for balance, his rope hand clenched to the braided line.

Most of the Mexicans sat together on a bleacher off to the side, and they all whistled and clapped and shook each other's hands.

Legs' score wasn't huge—a seventy-four—because his bull wasn't as homicidal as several others, so it required less gumption to ride. But when a rider lasted till the horn, and if he got away unscathed, that cowboy had earned a great victory. No person who actually saw it could believe otherwise.

Once the first round finished, the arena cleared and the judges made the draw for the championship round. Of the thirty-two riders, only nine had ridden to the horn. Ruben and I climbed off the catwalk and wandered over to the Mexicans, ranging from Humberto Juarez, a multi-millionaire who owned a shoe factory in Tecate, to rustic *frijoleros* who had snuck in through a hole in the fence. In Mexico, ricos like Juarez wouldn't be caught at a funeral with most of us, but in the arena they mostly hung together because they were Mexicans who had come to see Legs ride. I couldn't join the conversation because I wasn't wise to rodeo speak. Plus, I struggled to follow their rapid-fire Spanish.

Ferris Irons announced the draw and three thousand "Ooooohs" sounded from the crowd: Legs had drawn Vulcan. In the other bleachers, fans nodded their heads and shook their hands and whistled louder than when Miss Del Rio bounced through the arena on her big paint.

"*¡Joder!*" cursed a man beside me, pulling at his

moustache. "*Vulcan, pues*!"

"Who brought that bastard here?" Ruben asked.

"He'll kill our boy like he killed that gringo kid," said Humberto Juarez, shaking his fists toward the others.

"You think Legs will even try Vulcan?" someone asked.

"Sheeeeet yes, he'll try," Ruben said in English.

The Mexicans kept arguing over each other, not sure if Ruben's forecast was the best or worst news ever. Vulcan was a killer. Later, on the flight home, Ruben told me only three bulls in history had ever been more than five years on the circuit and never ridden to the horn. The other two were in the Rodeo Hall of Fame. In the past three years, Vulcan had killed one cowboy outright, and had maimed a dozen others. During the previous season, riders often suffered with groin pulls or bum elbows after drawing Vulcan. But this season nobody bothered feigning injuries: they refused to get anywhere near the bull. When word got out Legs was going to ride Vulcan, or try to, the mood grew ominous as we went to intermission.

Ruben and I climbed off the catwalk and walked to the food stands. The rider's score was accrued from both the bull's and the rider's performance, each having a possible max score of fifty points. The rankest bulls earned their riders high points, but also concussions, blown out knees and shoulders, broken arms, and buck-offs. "Thinning the heard," as Ruben called it.

The crowd pooled around the beer vendors and I wandered off to a quiet bench out by the tack house and started scribbling ideas in my notebook, searching out an angle for the documentary we never made because, despite a loyal fan base and long tradition, mainstream media considered bull riding a sideshow. How things changed. This long-forgotten Telemundo show was an early iteration of the Bulls-Only rodeos that, decades later, would pack venues from Madison Square Garden to the T-Mobile Arena in Las Vegas.

Soon after the Del Rio event, twenty-one cowboys gathered in a hotel room in Scottsdale, Arizona, and threw $1,000 each into a collective pot to fund the Pro Bull Riding Circuit. If you were one of the original investors in Professional Bull Riders, Inc., your seed money is now worth over $4 million in a sport broadcast into more than half a billion households in fifty nations and territories worldwide. But this was thirty years ago, when the overall winner took home a silver buckle and $2,500 cash money, and when bull riding clips were used as filler on late night cable, between cooking shows and *Bonanza* reruns.

They called it sport, even back then; but a proper documentary required some figurative theme to push Legs and bull riding into a larger context. Problem was, bull riding had no analogue because it didn't look, feel, or taste like anything else. The Roman Coliseum? The Great Pyramid of Tenochtitlan, where human sacrifices became an Aztec ritual? Maybe this Bulls-Only rodeo was a hayseed twist on a passion play, where cowboy messiahs faced life and death in the dirt. Jesus fought the Devil and was completed. The cowboys battled the cosmically rank bull, who had to be defeated, if only for eight seconds. I was reaching big, but this was Texas. Ferris Irons announced the bulls were running in fifteen minutes, and I hustled back to the arena, hoping I'd sorted out bull riding. I thought like that in my twenties.

The catwalk overflowed with photographers and a video crew from ESPN, plus a couple local news stations. The rock soundtrack kicked back in. Irons yelled, "Are we ready to rodeo?" and the crowd got rowdy again.

"Thank the Lord and grab your jewels, it's Shoat Tremble on Doctor Gizmo!"

And life was a blur once more, all streaking limbs and thundering hooves. A crash and burn, a perfect ride to the horn, another rider mashed into the fence, and the shrill wailing of ambulance sirens. No stopping now. The ESPN video crew flicked on some lights, and the cameraman bent over the guardrail, an assistant holding onto his waist. ZZ Top's "She's Got Legs" came over the PA, and the crowd erupted.

"Dad-burned right," said Irons. "We're talkin' 'bout *Señor* Legs on that son-of-a-biscuit, Vulcan, rankest beeve since the Forest Bull. So chain the dog and hide the kinfolk 'cause here comes Legs!"

The gate flew open and the audience roared but, for several seconds, the crowd on the catwalk stood in my way. Then Legs and Vulcan snapped into view, the killer bull looking like a giant eel fighting a riptide: writhing flanks, head, and limbs all convulsing north and south, up, down and sideways, with the violence of an electrocution. Corkscrewing in midair, hooves slamming into the dirt, pancaking Legs into its back. And Legs somehow stayed on-board. The beast was chocolate brown streaked with black, a grim and rippling hunk of heart meat that bolted to the center of the arena and whirred into a flat spin.

After about five seconds, the cheering drowned out the music. Vulcan vaulted and reared his head, scalding bolts of snot firing from his nose. Legs seemed nailed to the back of the creature. Once, both his legs flew over his head and his trunk doubled over so far to one side the bull's flank knocked his hat off. But Legs was still on-board, still over his rope hand, the bull and the cowboy melded together like a Minotaur. The horn sounded, but Legs and Vulcan were only starting to dance.

Vulcan broke into a bucking sprint, and Legs' rope hand was hung up. He tried loosing the lash with his free hand, clawing at the cinched rope between bounds, his boots trawling gullies through the dirt. But he couldn't break free. Twice they circled the arena, Legs flopping wildly, clawing at his hand, lashed in tight. Vulcan dug in and plowed to a stop. Legs flew over the horns, somersaulted, and landed about 30 feet away, his limbs splayed all over. A bullfighter dashed over, and Vulcan turned and chased him up the backstop fence (the arena doubled as a baseball park). The bull wheeled and rumbled after the other bullfighter, who dove into a big red barrel before Vulcan's lowered head crashed into it: the barrel sailed halfway to Amarillo before thunking back to the dirt.

The guy on the black horse dashed in and Vulcan charged straight at it. The horse ground into a turn and galloped away, sailed over the retaining wall at the far end of the arena and, unable to veer or completely stop, caromed off the Pepsi-Cola stand. The great bull pawed the dirt, shimmied, tossed its head, and finally hobbled off and slipped through the open gate into the back corral.

Legs lay face-down and didn't move. They cut the music. Everyone held their breath as the bullfighters raced over to Legs. Holding his side, and with a bullfighter on each arm, Legs finally teetered to his feet and stared at the sky, his mouth open and sucking air. Half the crowd clamored up the screen and hung by their fingers, screaming and rocking back and forth, nearly pulling the whole works down as the Mexicans stampeded over the rails and into the arena.

Someone jammed a sombrero on Legs' head and they paraded him around on shoulders to the strains of "She's Got Legs" cranked so loudly you could have heard it in the Yucatan. The other cowboys came into the arena and hoisted Legs in the air as well, and he tried to smile, though he kept clutching his rope hand, couldn't straighten, and mostly grimaced.

It took Irons ten minutes to clear the arena. They prodded Vulcan back inside where, despite favoring a leg, he snorted and feigned charges at the crowd, his savage breath mixing with the steam welling off his body. Every man, woman, and child pressed against the chain-link fence and gave the great bull a standing ovation. The cowboys were what the bulls made them, and Vulcan had made Legs a legend.

I noticed a rider, standing alone. He was big and lanky

with a loud, orange shirt, and Legs hobbled over and shook his hand. An old-timer there on the catwalk said the guy was traveling partners with the rider who'd died on Vulcan, several years before. The lanky guy stretched Legs' right arm over his shoulder and walked him back to the trainer's tent. Miss Del Rio, who'd changed into a gold lamé bodysuit, rode through the arena once more for good measure as the crowd, purged of a great tension, stood and cheered. Irons put his MC hat aside and said in plain English he and all the rest of us had witnessed history.

But we hadn't watched a passion play, or man-against-beast, or any of the other five-dollar ideas I'd cooked up while surfing adrenaline in Del Rio, when crowds were small and the purse modest and the half a billion viewers of the future had never heard of the George Paul Memorial Bull Riding challenge, or anything like it. It was blood sport, no question, but also a ritualized chance to flout the taboos and let our shadows rip, full-fucking-throttle. Miss Del Rio and baby Jesus, the great Devil bulls and stone cold crazy riders, blood on the dirt and ten beers in your gut, lust, violence, melodrama, machismo times fifty, corn pone sentimentality. All those passions that can shame our refinement and move us to tears, yet strangely reassure us that someone, somewhere is embracing the whole cosmic shitshow, for the length of a hot Texan night.

A couple weeks later, back in LA, Ruben told me D.J. Mulroon, who Black Ratchet had driven into the dirt like a tent stake, had a Grade Two concussion and was done riding bulls for the year. Surgeons screwed Buddy Dollarhide's ankle back together and he vowed to ride again next season. All the other riders who'd ridden the "meat wagon" out of the arena were back and riding again. But not Legs Maldonado, who'd ruptured several vertebrae while flopping around on Vulcan, and who doctors advised to quit bull riding forever. Vulcan, "the Secretariat of bucking bulls," had torn the big tendon in his hind leg.

"They retired each other," said Ruben.

N
NW
NE
W
E
SW
ES
S

SEASONS OF DROUGHT

MY BEATER VOLKSWAGEN VAN started slinging oil in Glenwood Canyon, but the engine sounded steady so I'd probably make it to my sister's place in Aspen. I downshifted, grinding gears, crested a rise, and rolled into a gray expanse, my headlights swallowed by the gloaming. A form arose on the dusky road, wobbling along the right shoulder and vanishing in my rear-view mirror. Something felt wrong, but I was afraid to stop and have the van die, so I cranked a U-turn and pulled alongside a guy, mid-twenties, missing a shoe and with a gash over one eye. A thin red rivulet trickled down his cheek. I parked on the shoulder, leaving the engine running, and jogged over to the guy, who kept lurching along the highway.

"Where you going?" I asked.

"Back to...The Ranch," he muttered. He reeked of liquor. Probably in a blackout.

"I oughta drive you."

I walked him back to the van and, through mumbled fragments, learned he'd driven his truck off the road and left it in a ditch.

"Better have a look," I said, unsure if I should search for his truck, drive him to a clinic, or what. I motored along the dark road, peering over my passenger, who kept burbling and dozing in turn. I spotted the truck in a bushy barranca just off the highway, suspended atop a bed of thorn scrub, lying upside down and pointed in the direction he'd come. The radiator steamed, the headlights were still on, and the front of the truck was mashed in as though he'd t-boned a telephone pole. No telling how he'd flipped from driving down a smooth embankment into a flat-bottomed ditch. Or took such a header and walked away with only a showy gash. No other cars were in sight. Nothing but empty highway, moonless sky, and grey chaparral rolling west toward the Elk Mountains.

The barranca was mostly dense hedgerow between patches of rubbly gravel and a few yellowing columnar trees. Shovels and rakes, chainsaws, red gas cans, coils of rope, and other tackle used in tree trimming and clearing land were scattered around the truck, wood handles poking from thorny limbs. My passenger started coming around. The truck was totaled. He could collect the tools in his own time. I climbed back into my van, wondering how I'd find The Ranch and get this over.

"You sure about this?" I asked when the passenger motioned toward a reddish dirt road, veering off the 82 and vanishing into the night.

"Quite," he said. "I used to live there."

He stuck his head out the window and threw up. I'd seen this happen during my football days and it usually meant a concussion. He'd probably been drinking for days. Jennifer would occasionally binge drink and, after this last time—when she did Fireball shots at a Nike event, and bitch-slapped the brand manager—I told her to just go back to Bogalusa. She wasn't supposed to actually go but, for fear of losing me, she'd quit boozing so hard and we could rattle on, hurling ourselves at another mountain to climb or river to run, each more reckless than the last, till the whole queasy tango flew apart.

The dirt road was well-traveled but sandy and went on and on, not a light in the distance, only the twin pikes of Mt. Sopris against black sky.

"Much further?" I asked.

"'Fraid so," he said, peering out at the silvered lines and magnificent distances, as if he and the valley went way back. I couldn't get a feel for this guy with our brief exchanges, so I guessed. His jeans, smeared with gear oil, made sense but the faded polo shirt didn't. The pearly smile meant braces, good dentists, and the money to pay for it all. He wore his long hair cinched back, and his features, nearly delicate, were set in quixotic curiosity.

I passed him my plastic water jug and he chugged without a breath and said, "Stream water." An hour before, I'd dunked the gallon jug in Woody Creek, where it spilled from the canyon and joined the Roaring Fork. My passenger held up the jug, eying the silt in the bottom.

"Got a name?" I asked.

"Nathanial," he said. He saw me grin at the fancy moniker and said, "Family name. I'm the reprobate." He took another long slug, grinned at the silt, and said, "Could almost pan this stuff."

I envied guys like this, with a main spring so bendy they can twist and bounce with anything, including a three-quarter-ton truck. Every Nathanial has a fable, a myth they're too busy living to tell you about, which deepens the charm and the bullshit. His gash needed a few stitches but the blood had dried on his cheek like a port wine stain and, in pale light, he took after a young Mikhail Gorbachev.

I pushed in a CD. Nathanial nodded at the music. "I've heard this."

"Bill Evans. My old girlfriend only left me a couple disks, so I pretty much know these songs by—"

"It's a nocturne," he offered.

Marvelous. A cultured tree trimmer. He'd puked on my van. I didn't like him, which he might have found amusing had I said so.

"You needn't have stopped for me."

"I always liked things to get out of," I said. "You figure it out."

He squinted into the shadows. "It's your next right."

The network of dirt roads suggested a grid, but we'd taken so many turns that finding my way back felt doubtful without map and compass, or a local. Finally, we pulled into a clearing jammed with 4x4s and European sedans, dusted with loam from the sandy drive-in. A ways off lay a hacienda-style ranch house and a halo of soft lights spilling over leisure stations—hanging lanterns and old sofas and chairs scattered about the concrete slabs. Country music blared from somewhere.

I parked, leaving the van running. Nathanial extended his hand and said, "Much obliged, man. You're a Huckleberry."

"Better get that cut looked at."

"Probably should," he said. I asked where I might refill my water jug and he pointed to the barn, out past the hacienda. Nathanial tipped an imaginary hat and walked away.

I pulled on the parking brake and made for the barn as a tall, athletic young woman with short braids walked past, bare feet shuffling through the sand, furiously chewing gum and smoking a blunt. She glanced up with a start. Her eyes were two black dots. A rail-thin guy with wild red hair and smeared raccoon eyeshadow burst from the dusk.

"Who are you?" he asked, staring. But before I could answer, he bolted.

Others appeared, most in their early twenties, little more than kids, wandering in circles. I knew the anxious cut of their jib: somebody, probably that morning, had busted out a load of mushrooms or a sheet of blotter acid, and the natives had shot for the stars. Now they were crashing back to earth, frying from the friction of re-entry.

Liquor wouldn't soften the landing, but Rachael (my name for her), short and sturdy as a wagon wheel, was trying, pacing the grounds with a half-drained fifth of Four Roses in her hand. She drew close and I wished she hadn't as the cadaverous stank of patchouli oil turned my stomach. Didn't bother the nebbishy little schlub—call him Harold—with a bling watch and suede loafers, hovering in Rachael's shadow.

"Do we know you?" said Harold, his mouth a twisted rictus.

"Just leaving," I said. The two weren't certain how to respond, or count to three, or tie their shoes. They'd likely followed the tacit pact I'd often seen between well-heeled parents and their castaway kids: so long as they beat it from public view their credit cards would keep working and they could balter through the fall, dropping acid and sneering at one another in fat-sorrow. I'd tried all that, without the credit cards, and might have cratered if Jennifer hadn't stuffed me into her Subaru and driven us out to Moab.

I jogged to the barn and started refilling the jug when up strode a cowboy Lothario so ace-high he might have starred in Rio Bravo. Even had the neckerchief.

"You bring Nathanial back here?" he asked. His eyes were bloodshot but he wasn't as gone as the others, and was probably the flahoolick who owned The Ranch, or whose family did. The crossed arms told me I owed him an answer.

"I picked him up on the highway," I said. "Right after—"

"Find him," said the Cowboy. "And leave." I finished filling the jug, screwed on the top as the Cowboy stepped closer. "You got me?"

"I'm going," I said. Prickly heat crept up the back of my neck. "But not with Nathanial."

The Cowboy stepped forward, blocking my way.

"I'll thrash him again," he said, "if you don't get him outta here."

Nathanial had to be one of them, but apparently was on the outs. He'd even profaned himself by taking blue-collar work. The scrap with the Cowboy made him untouchable. That was his problem. The Cowboy was now mine.

I hated tough guys. I'd grown up with one and had never

learned to handle them without trying to be one myself. When the Cowboy jabbed his finger in my chest, I swatted his arm away, dropped the water jug, and my right hand knotted into a fist. I was no kind of fighter but I was big, fit, and just clawing out of the wilderness. This was how people got hurt. Or dead.

Something made me stop, maybe the banality of us standing there glaring at each other like we cared, neither with a point worth making. A young woman, fine as a Vermeer, in a sleeveless yellow caftan, rushed up and shrieked, “Where’s Patty?”

The Cowboy spun toward the girl. “What about Patty?”

“She jumped in the bed of Nathanial’s truck, when he left,” the girl blurted. She grabbed at my arm and said, “Where is she? Where’s Patty?!”

The Cowboy charged over but his face had gone pale. I never thought to check the wreck for passengers.

“Nathanial drove his truck into a ditch back on the Eighty-Two,” I said, “maybe ten miles from Aspen.” Sweat was breaking over my face. “I can find it.”

The Cowboy and I jumped into his huge Ram truck and started barreling out the dirt road, powergliding around corners and slamming through ruts as we streaked toward scattered lights on the 82.

“He flipped his truck,” I said as we skidded onto the highway.

“Shit,” he mumbled. “Where?”

“Not far,” I said. “Better slow down.”

He gripped the wheel and kept gunning the truck, yelling and cursing to crush his fear. On this weekday in late August, between the summer art and winter ski crowds, the highway was mostly empty. I stretched out the passenger window, trying to spot the wreck in the black barranca. Nathanial's truck lights flickered; dim, but still on.

The Cowboy inched his truck off the edge of the road, several halogen pods beaming down at the wreck from the roll bar. We jumped out and piled down the hillside. The Cowboy kept shouting, "Patty!" as he burrowed into the thicket beneath the flipped truck, while I ranged around in a widening arc, parting branches, stomping over shrub and smarting from scratches, finding nothing but thorns, rakes, and gas cans.

One by one, other cars stopped on the road and jockeyed into position, high beams on, till the barranca gleamed like a dance floor. Maybe a dozen people—a young woman in running shorts and a Denver Broncos sweatshirt; a duffer in a suit and leather Oxfords; several guys in filthy orange coveralls, probably working on the new road opening in Basalt—peered down as I shouted up details. The woman plowed down into the barranca and the others followed.

The Cowboy kept kicking his legs, driving deeper into the thorn scrub below the wreck. The effect was instant and our little band fanned out. The guy in the suit, easily 60, was clearly all-in on a moment when life was made simple and clear: Find Patty. When he tore his slacks on the scrub, a guy off the road crew said, "We got this." The duffer looked slighted and the woman said, "He can buy other clothes."

Up on the road, a state trooper arrived and set out some flares as a few passing cars stopped along on the highway. I climbed the hillside to fill in the trooper. Trooper James listened soberly as I blurted details. A tow truck pulled over on the shoulder.

"We keep searching that scrub," said the trooper, after calling in backup from the Aspen PD. "If she doesn't turn up soon it'll mean she's underneath."

An ugly thought. But maybe Patty got tossed onto the shrubs and simply got her bell rung, and later, wandered into town.

"Not likely," said the trooper, "or we'd have found her by now."

"I guess you know these people," I said, as others from The Ranch trundled in.

The trooper glanced their way and said, "Yes, I do."

Ten minutes later we'd found no sign of Patty, so the tow truck backed to the edge of the road. The driver strung out some rusty cables and secured them to the far edge of Nathanial's truck.

It took three of us to drag the Cowboy from the scrub as he kicked and yelled, "That's my sister in there!" The woman and the old guy, who evidently knew the Cowboy, walked him over to a clearing while the red-headed crazy with raccoon eyes kept yelling stuff nobody could understand. Eventually, the trooper had his friends stick him in the back of a big camper van.

I moved over by the Cowboy and the old guy. Their shirts hung in tatters and thorns had slashed the Cowboy's face and arms. He glared into space and the woman in the Broncos sweatshirt said, "We'll find her."

The cables twanged tight. The tow truck shimmied, tires crabbing toward the ditch as one edge of Nathanial's truck started inching off the shrubs. The winch smoked and shrieked. The old guy yelled to clear out. We scattered seconds before the iron coupling connecting the cables blew apart. Shrapnel banged off the wreck and struck parked cars on the road. The cables bull-whipped back and blew out the rear window in the tow truck and cut the roof nearly in half. Nathanial's truck settled back right where it'd been.

Chaos. Several Aspen cops arrived and got busy wrangling traffic and rubberneckers, but could no longer keep the crowd away. Dozens lined the shoulder, including most of the waifs from The Ranch, glassy-eyed, biting their lips, a bad trip made heinous as others peered down in frantic dismay. We needed a plan.

The woman and old guy scrambled up the hillside and conferred with Trooper James, who directed all available trucks, along with four Aspen PD cruisers, to backtrack the dirt roads to The Ranch and check every turn and crook in case Patty had jumped or gotten launched. The rest of us would resume searching the shrubs and gravel patches, which we'd already combed through; but we welcomed the diversion while a mega tow truck, used to haul big rigs, drove in from El Jebel, 16 miles away.

The Cowboy dove back under the truck while we prowled the perimeter, bending back limbs, poking the brush with rake handles. If Patty was ever there we'd have found her long before. Rachael was somewhere. I could smell her. Harold had tagged along and furiously tried to tunnel through dense hedge below the front of the truck, getting ravaged by thorns and scalded by rusty sludge spewing from the radiator—and liking it. It was awful to watch and impossible to stop. Nobody tried.

The big tow truck had a massive chrome winch and the cables fed through a derrick-like structure mounted in back—an angle all the better for the hoist. It flipped over Nathanial's truck with ease and we swarmed over the empty imprint, finding nothing but a couple more rakes and gas cans. The Cowboy freaked, but no Patty meant she'd either jumped or had gotten thrown from Nathanial's truck on the drive out. Hurt, maybe. Probably. But surely not killed from tumbling into what amounted to a big sand lot.

Trooper James grilled the girl in the caftan who'd arrived with Rachael and had watched Patty jump into Nathanial's truck as he left the ranch. He seemed satisfied with her story and he sent the Cowboy and two more Aspen Police cruisers, lately arrived, to join the team scouting the dirt road. Others followed and the convoy vanished in a cloud. A sheriff's helicopter was blading in from Glenwood Springs, forty-five minutes away, to join the search.

The thrill had gone and the few others still loitering around the wreck shagged off while the Aspen cops ground out the flares and left to join the search on the sandy road.

Trooper James and I leaned against his cruiser. Aside from a random car passing every few minutes, the night was still as oil.

"Patty," I said, "whoever she is—"

"Her father runs the Citibank in town," said the trooper. "Or one of them banks. We might be done here, but this isn't over till we find her. We better join the others," he said, motioning me to get in the cruiser. But, on second thought, he walked us up the road and onto the shoulder, where tire tracks ran down into the barranca. He pointed to a large hole in the ground, webbed with roots, and panned his flashlight across the ditch, the beam settling on a big stump.

"He skids off the road and hits that stump," said the trooper. "Blows it right outta the ground, and the impact sends Nathanial flying. Explains why the front of his truck is stove-in." And why the truck lay perfectly centered on an untrampled island of scrub, as if lowered there by crane.

My eyes tracked a line from the stump to the truck, and beyond, wondering how far a body might fly if catapulted at speed. The trooper first spotted the tiny light flickering way out in the thorn scrub, far beyond where Patty might possibly have landed.

"Somebody ain't giving up," said the trooper.

I felt a jolt of shame that I had, and scrambled into the barranca, tromping through jungle and over to the flickering light—a tech headlamp, common to cavers and alpine climbers, which Nathanial wore strapped to his head. He stood knee-deep in the scrub, acknowledged me with a nod, and continued sweeping the scrub with the soft beam of his headlamp. He must have snagged a ride in with Rachael, or one of the others from The Ranch. As the rest of us searched where a person might be found, Nathanial trawled around out here like some rummy fishing for trout in the ocean.

I forded over to a gravel bar. How pathetic might this get—me stopping in the first place, driving a bloodied stranger in a time bomb van out miles of dirt roads, locking horns with a Cowboy sans cattle, onto a futile roundup for his sister, just to kill the lonely-fret of it all, finally hunkered in the toolies, not a star in the sky, as another lost soul called for Patty.

Nathanial kept poking the bushes, ranging farther out till he said, "Hello." His light had settled on a warped old 4x8-foot sheet of plywood. Could have been out there for years.

"That's from the back of my truck," he said.

I didn't see how; but maybe once he'd gone airborne the plywood found a gust and frisbeed way out here. No matter. Nathanial's truck was toast and the oily old board was trash. Nevertheless, he struggled to wrestle the board from the shrubs and I finally lent a hand rather then watch him flailing around.

Branches trapped the edges of the plywood and it took us several tries to muscle it free. Lying underneath, flat on her back on the hedgerow, was Patty, staring up in a liminal trance, moving her lips but making no sound.

Shock. Aside from a few scrapes on one arm she didn't have a mark on her.

Nathanial grabbed her hand and said, "Patty Cakes, you silly girl. You should have let me go." She tried to sit but winced. Nathanial gently pushed her back and said, "We'll go get something to carry you up to the road."

Her eyes flashed and she said, "Don't leave me!"

"Tried that already," he said. "Didn't work."

"I'll be right back," I said.

"You're shittin' me," said Trooper James, gaping off at Nathanial's headlamp. "Gotta be fifty feet past the wreck."

"I'm thinking more."

Paramedics hefted Patty into a wooden backboard because she couldn't walk out. A broken hip, they thought, but no spinal damage or other apparent injuries. They'd know more later. The crew searching the dirt road had returned as well and, when the Cowboy saw Nathanial, tempers boiled over till the old man stepped between them. Nathanial had gone out by himself, he said, and found his sis while they were chasing a wild goose around those dirt roads. Things cooled, a little. They loaded Patty into the ambulance. The Cowboy handed me the key to his truck and said, "Your van's back at The Ranch. Wait for me there." He almost smiled at the trooper and said, "Getting tired of us yet?"

"Better get something for those scratches," said the trooper. "You look like shit."

The Cowboy and Nathanial crammed into the

ambulance and it wheeled off, followed by trucks and cars and people touched by the fugacious grace of chance. The Aspen cops drove off in different directions, leaving the trooper and I and the Cowboy's big Ram truck on the side of the road.

"Couple hours ago," I said, "I felt like killing that cowboy."

"His folks might have paid you to do it," said the trooper. He handed me a business card with a gold, seven-point star—the seal for the Colorado State Troopers. He'd have to write up the whole adventure and made me promise to fill in the beginning, since he wasn't there.

"No worries," I said, and slipped the trooper's card into my wallet.

Next day, I jotted out a couple pages of notes on a legal pad, got distracted, and stuck the pages in a *Time Life* photo book I'd bought in a thrift store. That's where they stayed till last week when, bored as hell from the Covid quarantine, I discovered them while decluttering a bookcase in my shed. Years of storage had curled the edges, but I could still make out the words. My apologies to Trooper James Della Cruz for not writing this out till now.

"I will greet the sun again
and the little river that once ran in me
and the clouds that were my ruminations,
my companions in those seasons of drought."

- Forough Farrokhazad

A BEND IN THE RIVER

BLACK SMOKE SPEWED THROUGH holes in the ship's open deck, so gouged and corroded and cobbled with pig iron patches if a single spot weld ever let go, the entire quaking heap would stove-in on itself and sink. The pilot was all leather and bones and his gaze had the set changelessness that comes from years of silence and solitude. He rarely spoke. When the engine started clanking he grunted to his caboclo (the mixed-race river people of the lower Arce) assistant, maybe 13 years old, who once more ducked below. Hammering rang from the hold. The engine hit its clunky rhythm and the boy crawled back on deck, hacking from the smoke, smeared with grease and reeking of bilge and benzene. Whenever he wasn't toiling on the engine, he worked a hand-cranked bailer every waking minute. He had a long lick of shiny black hair and strips of tire thonged to his feet. He hadn't eaten a thing but saltines during our two days on the barge.

The deck overflowed with fuel drums, cases of Pepsi-Cola, canned foods, rebuilt outboard motors, rolls of Visqueen and sheet metal, even a plastic Christmas tree dusted with snow, ordered by the dwindling outposts, plantations, and native settlements upriver. The human cargo had thinned to the pilot, the boy, Dwight, and me. This was my eleventh trip to the wild places with Dwight, who I'd grown up with in Southern California, who would go anywhere at any time and enjoyed discovering, somewhere along the way, why we had gone in the first place. Our last few adventures were our best because we started with so little, drawn to an obscure river by a sepia photograph in an old book written in Dutch, or by a curious-sounding village or tribe which nobody knew much about. Family and friends were vexed why the moment we had time and funds we once more were getting typhoid boosters and Recombivax shots and scrounging visas to Kalimantan, New Hebrides, and now, Brazil. How could we, well into our thirties, disentangle ourselves from our peers, and the quest for significant stuff, and up and go? I was a nobody from nowhere. But Dwight came from money so big, abandoning the castle made him a traitor, betraying the ways and means of a life that mattered. We could never give them reasons why, in those moments, they didn't.

Late that afternoon, as the barge took on more fuel, we trudged through the mud, heading for the mine we'd read about in *Época*, a popular weekly magazine we'd filched from the bar at the São Paulo International Airport, on our flight from Caracas, Venezuela, to Brazil the previous week.

The pilot and kid stayed on-board, doing small repairs. The kid had spent more than a year mired in the mine, basically a child slave, before the pilot found him and pulled him out. Their business was upstream. We had an hour before the barge hammered on.

The miners had razed the jungle for five square miles, the fringe a jumbled chaos of bulldozed trees crackling with flames and hissing in the deluge. Raw sewage clashed with the ripe smell of worked earth as we approached a seething sump full of ex-cons, ex-barbers, ex-doctors, even ex-priests. The racket swelled and the smoke thickened as we trudged closer to the massive open pit and peered inside. 200 feet below were an estimated forty thousand itinerant prospectors—*garimpeiros*—nearly naked, glazed in sweat and muck and rain, one thunderous livid mudhole of flashing shovels and writhing backs attacking a sloppy grid of claims averaging 20 square feet. A dozen men, hip to hip, worked each tiered plot. We saw workers slither into holes while others were dragged out by their ankles, bags of dirt clutched in their hands as, all around, men shoveled, swung axes and mauls, and levered huge stones with pry bars. I watched a man turn to piss and get a pickax through his foot. The two men fought and one opened the other's forehead to the bone. A dozen others piled on, but the surrounding throng hardly noticed and never stopped.

A train of roughly five thousand men trudged through the mud in an endless loop, shouldering enormous burlap bags of soppy soil up a steep slope, legs shin-deep and churning, finally stumbling to the summit mound of tailings and dropping their bags and collapsing as if dead except for their heaving ribs. Others, also by the thousands, hunched under huge wet sacks and practically standing on each other's shoulders, teetered up a web of creaky bamboo ladders, some 50 feet high, linked via crumbling terraces. They stumbled to the top and dumped their bags, the sloppy paydirt sluiced and panned by ten thousand other men while the carriers, sheathed in muck, rose wearily and joined the loop for another load. Each task done by hand, the toil and wretchedness heightened by taskmasters screaming at the workers, who had little chance of unearthing the big ingot, and no chance of getting paid until they did. Forty thousand muddy men sustained by jungle tubers and coconut juice and the handful of millionaires strutting around the mud.

One of them, featured in *Época*, was Guilhermino Caixeta, the 23-year-old son of subsistence farmers from Cuiabá. He'd dug out a nugget big as an attaché case, somehow escaped the mud hole with his life and the ingot, and bought a *rancho* in Borba with twelve thousand head of cattle. Even gave his folks a job. As peons. Guilhermino had since returned to the mine owing to *febre do ouro*, gold fever, a soul sickness healthy people streamed in from all four corners, hoping to catch. Cocaine fueled the operation, and most everyone in it. Jacked by the drug, men could eat less and work longer. Narcos controlled the trade until the military took over the mine the previous Easter. Now it was open war between the two, the brass cashing in either by strong-arming their cut or simply confiscating the blow and having junior officers peddle it directly to the miners. Freelancers trying to deal the generals out of their cut were given two options: take a bullet to the head, or deal for the generals. But no matter, said *Época* in a lurid cover story. The blow would keep flowing over the Bolivian divide and up the river so long as there was a *cruzeiro* to buy it and gold to be had. "Guernica," without the bombs.

We paced along the muddy perimeter, peering into the sump, my eyes searching out Guilhermino Caixeta, the peon miner and multimillionaire. He had to be down there somewhere, laughing, colossal nuggets in both hands. But all the faces swam together into a mirror image of my own dislocation. Out beyond the swamp and the blazing shoal of trees, Dwight shuttered photos of a spoonbill perched in a solitary jacaranda tree, peering at a wilderness no soul or God could endure. Only the *garimpeiros* could. Somewhere down there was their redemption. Somewhere down there was gold.

We forded back to the barge, trailing a string of caboclo kids—too wasted or broken to continue in the mine—and pushed on upriver, hour by hour offloading our cargo of young refugees. Most had been driven downstream by poverty, or curiosity, even indentured as the result of a father's dice game with the miners—and thrown straight into the pit. They were surrounded by strangers and a strange language, fed strange food, made to work like animals. Often they sickened, collapsed, were sometimes beaten. And since dying in the pit ruined morale, they'd get shunted back upstream, worse off than when they arrived and rarely one *cruzeiro* richer. They'd stumble off the boat at the vaguest shoals, find a footpath, and meld into the fastness, never looking back.

Two days above the mine we passed the last boat scouring the riverbed for gold. Another day and we passed the last miner and the final logging camp and forged into primary terrain. The forest reared higher, the river narrowed, the current quickened, the boat slowed.

We hugged the bank against the current and plied through curtains of green light slanting from the trees. The caboclos called it *el salón verde*, the green room. Gnarled ropes looped down dangling in midair, flecked with black orchids and strangler figs. Bullfrogs croaked from fetid streams emptying into the river. Twice we passed mangrove coves bellowing the mad chorus of howler monkeys. Every few hours we'd chug past a small settlement marked by the sparse, meager homes of the caboclos. Their thatched hovels, set high on wooden piles, overlooked the river from above the monsoon line. Now and again the pilot would veer around islets of rushes in the river shallows, his hands slow dancing with the giant ship's wheel. I milled around the stern, smoking Brazilian cigarettes and staring into the trees. This was likely my last sortie into the wild places, at least into the beating heart of it. The caboclos ventured downstream. We were going up, seeking a different life. If only we went far enough, we'd molt out of ourselves and fly.

The engine clanked like hell. The pilot, fighting the current, pulled over at a small, abandoned settlement half a mile upstream, and tied off to a cannonball tree at the waterline. Several decaying, oblong huts stood on palm pylons in the small clearing. The pilot and the boy worked below while we panted in the bow, soon forced off the boat when the top end of a grimy diesel engine covered the open deck. The pilot mumbled a few sentences, motioned toward the huts, handed me a sledgehammer, and went back below to the hammering. Portuguese was close enough to Spanish I usually caught the gist.

"He says the sun's going fast and they need a fire to work by," I told Dwight. "He's got to make Raul by Thursday and can't waste a day on repairs. We can get the wood off those huts."

"What about the people?" Dwight asked. I glanced toward the huts.

"The pilot said they all died last year. Measles."

We climbed a notched log and into the first hut, sobered by the wooden basin intricately braided into the reed wall, a carved stool, a manioc grater leaning in the corner, as if carelessly left there yesterday. We went back outside and laid into the hut with the sledgehammer. In an hour, we had a growing pile of bamboo, reeds, and hardwood joisting, and a fire licking 30 feet into the air.

The sky was dark and starless. All night the pilot and the boy tinkered with the engine, and all night Dwight and I worked the fire to keep the light high enough to slant into the boat, our shadows dancing over the somber screen of trees. My eyes were occasionally drawn to the prow of the barge, where a brass nautical figurehead, one of Neptune's angels, was welded in place, her features so gouged by collisions and deep green rust she couldn't possibly see us. But I kept checking to make sure, feeling like a grave robber as we bashed away.

The wood gave out in the wee hours, and Dwight and I took turns sledgehammering the palm pylons until they worked loose and we could draw them from the gluey soil and roll them into the fire. The engine fired over and the pilot waved us back aboard. Behind us, a mound of coals smoked and crackled. In a week, the rising current would claim the cinders and the jungle would creep over the small clearing. Rain and wind would salt the ruin and, in a matter of months, there would be nothing but a solitary pylon to tell a traveler that people had lived and died here.

Rain beat down from one black cloud, the blood-red

sun beside it. Steam welled off the moving water—dull, hanging, and so thick I could taste my own hot breath. Thunder clapped through the green corridor, followed by sheets of blistering rain.

The river surged a foot in fifteen minutes, and fifteen minutes later the sun filled half the sky. The barge rattled on, the pilot's face pouring sweat and fixed upriver, like a man stalked from behind. Everything here was stalked from behind, from downriver. The forest grew close and immense and the slender aisles between trees darkened.

Towards sunset the sky caught fire between rags of clouds and the river, flat and still, shined like liquid gold. A tribesman paddled by, a huge manatee in the floor of his dugout canoe. The tribesman's chin was smeared red with annatto and, on both sides of his face, a tattooed streak ran from the corners of his mouth to his temple. He neither ignored nor acknowledged us, slowly riding the current downstream, the huge mammal's tail twitching and flashing in the light. We walked along the barge all the way to the stern, watching the tribesman until, far in the distance, he fused with the flaming water. The day, hour by hour, seemed to dissolve into the river. I'd scribble in my journal, fold it shut mid-sentence, and stare into the forest gliding by.

For most of a decade, since fleeing "The Ditch"

(Yosemite Valley), my journal described a succession of exotic beatdowns consequent to chasing some feat or discovery: a first traverse, a first contact, an unexplored cave or uncrossed jungle or most any damn thing which sounded novel and risky and could affirm our repute as adventures, as bolder than you'll ever be, as seeing things you'll never see. But as the fog burned off came the slow realization I'd been living for some years in a bubble. My life spanned the globe—I had two ten-page extensions in my passport, with stamps from Bougainville to the North Pole—but my world was much smaller than I'd ever imagined. I'd have to learn how to stay put for my life to expand and burst the bubble. But I couldn't settle.

We made it to the outpost at Quejos early the next day. Another small, grimy barge onloaded fuel drums on its journey downstream. Dwight and I helped the boy roll off half their cargo, and the pilot steered the barge back into the current. The deck lay bare except for several fuel drums, three pallets of various foodstuffs, and the plastic Christmas tree. Who ordered the thing? They must have come from where the love light gleams, which was always somewhere else. We watched the little settlement recede. A bend in the river, and the world behind us disappeared.

Three miles upstream, the river pinched and steepened into a gutter of spume, roiling holes, and standing waves. We drove straight into the creaming tide, veering around sandbars and shoals, grating over river shallows as water-logged trees torpedoed the prow. In two weeks, the returning monsoon would raise the waterline five feet or more, but now, in low water, we butted boulders and battled swirling eddies, fighting for a precarious course.

A hydra of roots and lianas entangled the prop, and the pilot throttled down before the seizing engine blew apart. As the current plowed the barge downstream, the pilot dashed forward and threw off a huge, rusty anchor, which dragged and skipped along the river bottom and finally caught with a lurch, the straining chain nearly tearing the strut off the deck.

The pilot lashed a rope around the boy's waist and Dwight and I braced to belay him from the helm, our legs stemmed out between crates on the iron deck. The boy grabbed a machete, drew a lungful, and dove underwater. A faint ticking sound on the prop, and a mass of black vines floated to the surface and washed downstream. The boy's head burst through the foam, and he gulped half the sky in panicked mouthfuls before the current pulled him back under. We pulled harder still to reel him back into the boat.

The anchor gave way and the boy disappeared underwater as the barge swirled sideways to the current, water gushing over the deck. Dwight and I scrambled back to the stern and hauled the boy in. He collapsed on deck like a big brown fish bound in roots and creepers, hacking and wheezing, water streaming from his nose. Dwight beat on his back until he heaved and hacked some more and started breathing right.

The pilot slammed the old barge into gear and battled to gain an upriver line as I returned to the bow and cranked the anchor back on board. Onward we went, careening off rocks, grinding through snags, Dwight beside me at the bow, scouting and yelling out obstacles. The moment the boy caught his breath, he dashed below, hammering like a railroad coolie as the old pilot coaxed the rust bucket upstream. And so it went the entire day.

Near sunset, the river leveled off, and on both sides the green hedgerow ran straight ahead, a long, hushed foyer tapering into the night. Far in the highlands, outlined one against the other, the crests of a high cordillera were shuffled like a deck of stony cards—brusque peaks, bluish draws, jutting arêtes swaying and rising and falling in the harsh light, ever more inaccessible as we motored on. The pilot maneuvered to the middle of the sleeping river, now 100 feet across. Dwight lowered the anchor. A mile ahead were more cataracts, said the pilot, and the three hours between us and the next settlement were the trickiest yet. He'd need all the daylight to navigate this stretch. We moored for the night.

The whole sky fell all at once. Through the rainy gray pane the land loomed void and dark. The deck swirled shin-deep. We stripped to shorts and stood in the bow, the hot rain streaming over us as we stared at rain pocking the water, and at the buffeting limbs of the plastic Christmas tree. The pilot took great care with the tree, never brushing its snowy limbs while offloading drums and crates, and checking its lashings several times a day.

The new moon burned off the inky water. An electric silence fell around us and the feeling of pure duration. The pilot gestured toward the left shore and said, "Urupa." Two forms came into focus, and we saw these ghostly shapes were alive, squatting on their heels, their faces cast in irrefutable sneers. Somewhere in the bush around them lurked their clansmen, the dusky, bleeding sacrifices of an industrial juggernaut adding nothing to the beauty of their land or the life of their souls. "Wilderness," which had always indicated the original and untrodden, increasingly suggested black magic acts of disappearance. In a few years, the world around us—the trees, the natives, *El Salon Verde* itself—would vanish forever.

Under a pattern of stars, the pilot broke into a pallet and opened two canned hams. We ate thick slices offered to us on the tip of the pilot's stiletto, and watched the boy devour the entire second ham with his bare hands, jellied fat streaming from the corners of his mouth.

N
NE
E
ES
S
SW
W
NW

KING KONG COMES TO WABAG

DWIGHT POINTED TO A BLURB headlined with: "Two Die in Enga Fight." He flipped me the newspaper and I skimmed the story.

"Two men died of ax and arrow wounds on Friday after a fight broke out between Lyonai and Kundu tribesmen outside of Wabag, in Enga Province. Joseph Yalya, 38, of Pina Village, died of an ax wound to the neck, and Tumai Tupigi, also of Pina Village, died from an arrow through the chest. Police said about eight hundred men were involved in the fight. The brawl began when Lyonai tribesmen accused the Kundu clan of using sorcery to kill a Lyonai elder."

Two casualties sounded modest for an eight-hundred-man melee, but Papua New Guinea plays by its own rules, and both tribesmen and travelers stumble around in a daze, half astonished, half bored. Dwight and I had gone there strictly for the hell of it, looking for novelty while licking wounds after a nine-week exploratory thrash down the Strickland Gorge. I'd worked and scrimped and flown to world's end, hacked through that hateful gully for all those weeks hoping to discover the Lost Tribe of Levi, only to stumble out the ass end with little more than dysentery. But after two days slumming around Mount Hagen in the remote Highlands, we hankered for another epic. We had eight days before our flight to Sydney, then onto California, so it had to be a quick one. One look at the newspaper article and our prospects brightened.

We snagged a ride from Solomon Chang, a tightly wrapped engineer of Chinese-Papuan parentage, driving to a reservoir project, 20-something miles past Wabag.

The road, called the "Highland Direct," was straighter than the Oregon coastline, but rockier, which gave Chang nearly five hours to ramble on about native "warfare."

"The buggers spill onto the road sometimes," said Chang, who'd spent his school days in Sydney, Australia. "But they'll usually stop for cars. Maybe bum a smoke or two. And I've never seen them fight through lunch, neither." So, some histrionics accompanied this combat, though, according to Chang, someone eventually had to die "to keep the contest real." We had a solid week to get into trouble. Chang had that night but liked his chances.

We wheeled into Wabag, hoping to duck a salvo of spears and arrows, and instead wandered past the same old tumbledown grass huts and through the shambling open-air market. This *lic lic ples*, or small place, teamed with Kanakas dressed in "ass-grass," a patch of kunai grass in front and back secured with a thick leather belt. Each man carried an ax over their shoulder and had feathers or boar tusks pierced through their septum. And, as always, every jowl bulged with betel nut and rancorous red spit. We were right back to swatting mosquitoes again, but our boredom paled compared to Chang's.

"Look," said Chang, "we ferret out some chief and make off with his daughters." He considered for a moment. "Better yet, his pigs. That'll get the machetes flashing."

A few weeks before, miles into bumfuck, a native sorcerer got hold of Dwight's tiny MP3 player, and thought we'd crammed the spirits of his dead relatives into the device, torturing them with trumpets and electric guitars. Not our finest moment, and we stressed the need to proceed cautiously with cultures we didn't fully appreciate.

"Leave off with your travel guide bullshit," said Chang. "I was born here, for chrissakes." A long silence. I could hear the gears grinding in Chang's head. "OK, it's Saturday. We'll swing by the bar, then hoof it over to the theater for *King Kong Meets Godzilla*."

"Followed by a little Schubert on bamboo instruments," said Dwight. Wabag didn't have a store, so how could it have a theater?

"I'm on the square here," said Chang. "It's been Kong and Godzilla every Saturday night for two years. But it's not the flick that's the draw, but the Kanakas. Most believe they're watching a documentary. They'll hike all the way in from the Gulf Province to screen it."

We checked into the Wabag Lodge, an open-air dive with "running bath" (the river), and headed for the bar—a double chain-link cage, with a cashier and stock of South Pacific Lager inside. We paid first, and they fed the bottles through a little slot in the fencing. We drank a couple and made for the theater, following a dark path to a small clearing in the otherwise impenetrable thicket.

The theater (the "Wabag Ritz," as Chang called it) described a converted cement garage used previously to store the province's three John Deere tractors. A noisy queue of Kanakas passed through the tiny entrance. Dressed exclusively in ass-grass, everyone had to check in their axes and machetes, receiving a numbered bottle cap to reclaim them. Several men, apparent newcomers to the Ritz, were confused by this procedure, but worked things out with the enormous native official at the front door. He, too, wore the ass-grass, but also a creased khaki shirt and a red beret on his billowing bouffant. He flashed a wide smile at seeing Chang.

"*Sainaman tru.*" This from the giant.

"*Strongpela tru,*" Chang came back. The two exchanged a five-move handshake. Chang turned toward Dwight and me and said, "*Dis pela se mi prem bilong mi.* Americans."

"Oh, how ya doing?" the giant said fluidly in Aussie-accented English. "You best grab a seat while you can." We went in.

Seventy-five tribespeople pressed inside. Various benches lay half empty as many Kanakas chose to squat in the oily dirt. The whitewashed front wall served as the screen. The ancient projector sat askance on a bamboo stand. The heat withered, but the aroma could have turned the stomach of the Discus Thrower. The Kanakas' diet consists largely of forest tubers and manifold shrubbery, and they continuously pass a crippling wind, unabashed and most sonorously. Blend this with knee-buckling body odor and the fetid stench of betel nut expectoration, box it all in a ventless concrete sarcophagus, and you have the Wabag Ritz.

"Swank joint, eh?" said Chang.

"Probably no worse than the atmosphere on Mercury," I said.

"*Pasim tok*," the giant barked, and the crowd slowly quieted. He flipped on the projector, which made a gnashing noise like someone feeding hubcaps into a wood chipper. He compensated by cranking the volume, which distorted the dialogue beyond anything human, but rendered King Kong that much more impressive. As Kong stomped through Tokyo, swatting skyscrapers and feasting on pedestrians, their legs flailing in his jagged teeth, the mob shrieked and many Kanakas dove beneath the benches, cowering and trembling and babbling about the "*bikpela monki, em i kaikai saipan man*."

During the scene when Godzilla and Kong had it out, a fight erupted in the corner. A riot seemed likely till one Kanaka swung her bilum bag of tubers upside another Kanaka's head, and all eyes returned to the wall. Then a courageous Kanaka stole up to the screen to "touch" Godzilla. He turned around, squinting into the light and got bombarded by sweet potatoes and betel nut husks. He screamed, the crowd howled, the giant barked, and the bushman bolted back to his bench.

The end credits rolled out and the wall went dark. Silence. Then shouts for more. The giant yelled, "*No gat*," but the crowd wouldn't have it. So, to avoid a sure riot, he rolled the film back in reverse. As King Kong backpedaled through Tokyo, withdrawing reconstituted pedestrians from his snapping jaws and placing them back on the sidewalk, Dwight, Chang, and I were right there with the Kanakas, all up on our feet and waving our arms, ducking spuds, screaming, and cheering at the miraculous events dancing on the whitewashed wall.

SHOOTING THE TUBES

WE PLANNED ON AN early start but Carlitos got hijacked by a telenovela marathon about a young heartthrob named Figaro, who stumbled across a smashing nun named Roseanna. Then Roseanna's half-brother, the profligate rancher, Julio Del Monte, came to visit, having recently been swindled out of six hundred Belgian Blue beeves by Figaro's stepfather, Don Plutarco Rincon. A fire broke out and the plot took off, but we didn't, not leaving the Hotel Maravillas until going on midnight, when we rolled out of Caracas in a rusty Chevy Biscayne.

Early the next morning, we sputtered into El Tigre, a ghetto town on the upswing, sprawled across scalding savannah carpeted in range grass and flecked with bushy Moriche palms. A decade later Venezuela nationalized their *petro* industry, but back then, the rigs were largely managed by *Yanqui* engineers holed up in vast, hermetically sealed *campamentos*. The mercury sizzled at 95 in the shade, if you could find any.

The moment we arrived at Carlitos' family home, 300-pound Abuelita stopped kneading the *arepa*, quavered to her feet and kissed Carlitos, her very grandson, on the lips as his arms went stiff and he bicycled his sneakers away. Niece Pepina, six-foot-one and thin as a cactus quill, rushed over with a tray of pig's feet *al carbón* as a dozen rowdy kids sprang from nooks and cubbies. A home in Venezuela is rarely short on kids. The people pride themselves on getting married when they want, not when they should, and they quickly fashion a couple *niños* because they can. I was the first gringo to enter their house—or their neighborhood—during my first visit the previous Easter. But so long as I was Carlitos' friend, and now Teresa's fiancé, the house, and everything in it, was mine.

We slept till dinnertime, when brother Luis Manuel rushed in from work, cowboy hat perched just above his dark eyes, a chrome starter pistol in his hand. Thick, mustachioed, with a face you've seen on post office fliers, Luis Manuel worked sixty-hour-a-week shifts at the petrochemical plant outside Anaco to preserve the dignity of the household. He bolted past Carlitos and me into the *jardín* to fire three glorious rounds (blanks) into the sky. Then he laid down several Creole dance steps, booted a sleeping dog, cracked his bullwhip, fired a fourth blank at me, and slapped my back till I gasped.

His black eyes narrowed. "*Matrimonio? Cuando?*"

When I mentioned a tentative date for the wedding, Luis Manuel hugged me, Pepina, Carlitos, finally Abuelita, and he broke back into his dancing, faster this time. My first time in El Tigre I swore Luis Manuel was putting all this on, like a crazy uncle in a Latino cartoon. Only when I spied him all alone and acting just as uncorked did I know he came this way. He once more made for his pistol, halted by a bottle of *Doña Bárbara*—a bathtub shine that could strip the hide off a dinosaur—proffered in Abuelita's plump hand. He swilled a tan inch before Pepina snatched it back for Abuelita to lock in a chipped wooden cabinet secured with a single key, the silver skeleton Abuelita tucked into her black lace brassiere, a fallow acre no human, sober or drunk, would dare trespass.

We all sat down and feasted through flanks of *bistec*, fried plantains, *ensalada aguacate*, crunchy sheets of *casabe*, quarts of *jugo de tamarindo*, and various colorful tubers with impossible names. Later, Abuelita got a headache, requiring a trip to the *farmacia* for headache medication, a journey of nearly five blocks. Luis Manuel could have walked there and back in ten minutes, but he took the pickup—because he had one, because it had a full tank, because he'd washed and waxed it on the weekend, and because, when he gunned it, which he normally did, it roared like the cannons at Pampatar. All this made the man appear all the more *magnifico* as he thundered down the street to the cheers of friends leaning in doorways and lounging on their verandas.

Going to the *farmacia* in the pickup was an event, and an event in El Tigre, no matter how big or small, is always performed in numbers. I wedged myself into the bed of the pickup among a dozen kids, several dogs, and Abuelita, whom Luis Manuel, Carlitos, and I conveyed there in an easy chair, and who would check the expiration date on the medication to ensure it was *bueno*. As Luis Manuel gunned the truck down the road, frame sagging to the pavement, the great straight pipes belching three-foot flames and whoops sounding from every porch and open door we passed, I reentered the emphatic world of a people who lived like everybody would if they could ever stop worrying about life and just live it.

Back in the house, as I watched a red gecko creep across

a peeling white wall, Luis Manuel laid out his plan. Or started to.

"*Guacala*! What now?" Carlitos moaned. As I later learned, Luis Manuel's plans often ended in spectacular debacles, including bulldogging range donkeys, a stunt costing Luis Manuel several teeth and a fractured collarbone; salsa dancing with the mayor's wife, resulting in jail time and a flogging for Carlitos; and paddling a canoe after the truculent Yajiros, the local indigenous tribespeople, into the darkest jungle and getting lost for three days.

"*Disparando a los tubos*," said Luis Manuel.

"Shooting the tubes?" said Carlitos.

"*Sí, chamo.*" And Luis Manuel explained. During construction of the nearly completed hydroelectric plant in Tascabana, 30 miles outside town, the Cariña Indians had discovered tube-shooting through accident. The plant's cooling system required rerouting several surrounding rivers, accomplished via five-foot-diameter steel tubes piping water along a twisting path to a central aqueduct, where it drained into the plant and exited to a river below. *Disparando a los tubos* involved intentionally performing what had mistakenly happened to a young Cariña boy who, while diving for crayfish, got drawn into a half-filled drainage tube and became a human torpedo, tearing in black passage for several hundred feet before his free-fall exit into the open aqueduct.

To give us a clear picture, Luis Manuel, who'd punished a

covert bottle of licorice cordial for several hours, assumed various dive-bomb positions on the cement floor until he spotted a terrific *cucaracha* on the wall, a three-incher, black as sin. He sprang for his bullwhip, but Pepina thrust out her pool cue leg and tripped him. The roach zipped into a chink in the wall and the roof nearly blew off for all the laughing, none louder than Abuelita, who farted like a big rig backfiring. The key to the liquor cabinet bounced from her dress and clinked on the floor. Luis Manuel dove for the key, but got only a handful of Pepina's moccasin. Grandmamma repositioned the key back in no man's land, broke wind once more, and we all just cleared the hell out.

Luis Manuel fanned himself with his hat and spit like a real man, pining that tomorrow's tube-shooting would be the last of it. Foundry workers would weld grates over the tubes' entrances before the plant powered up on Monday. Since Teresa wouldn't arrive in El Tigre till the following evening, tube-shooting sounded fine by me. The chickens were roosting and *Doña Bárbara* was finished. Luis Manuel grabbed his bullwhip to hunt for *cucarachas*.

We headed out for Tascabana and the tubes the next morning, rumbling through a scattering of drowsy pueblos. On the outskirts of San José de Guanipa rose an adobe shack topped by a peeling icon, gaudy as a circus bill, featuring a ravaged Jesus dragging the cross toward

Golgotha. Several Roman soldiers were whipping Our Savior who, under a crown of thorns big as a tractor tire, stumbled on, drenched in blood. A long line, mainly children and old women in mourning, filed in one side of the shack and out the other.

"For fifty bolivars, you can get in line to see part of Jesus's genuine crown of thorns," said Carlitos.

"Is that a fact?" I said, craning my neck to study the grisly icon.

"But it's only a small part," Carlitos added. "Over in Falcón they got a whole one."

"*Verrrrrga*!" Carlitos yelled as Luis Manuel wheeled his pickup toward the mob at Tascabana. Easily five hundred people were already there. Some had driven from as far away as Ciudad Bolívar. Others had ridden burros for hours across blazing plains to shoot the tubes, or to drink, or both. The city council and the National Guard had decreed various safety procedures, all ignored, and a phalanx of soldiers stood by to try and enforce them.

From atop two jalopies parked on opposite banks of an Olympic pool-sized mudhole, the mayor of Tascabana (Don Armando Brito, renowned for reading nothing except Marvel Comics and the Bible) and one Lt. Colonel Juan Baltazar Negron megaphoned commands, sounding like crazed hyenas. Easily one hundred cars, stereos blaring, girded the sump in a formation so tight Luis Manuel, Carlitos, and I had to tread over trunks, roofs, and hoods to gain the mudhole. At the waterline, local kids hawked sweet bread and bottled pop while, on small patches of surrounding dirt, people barbecued chickens, fatty sausages, and pig rinds for their beloved *chicharrones.* The sun beat down like a hammer, and a fetid brume of sweat, charcoal smoke, burning pig fat, and toilet water (Venezuelans love their cologne) hung over the lagoon, which floated more trash than a World Cup soccer stadium.

Enriched by dollar-a-liter booze, the mob laughed, jeered, and shouted, anxious to go before their valor washed downstream. Bobbing pop cans, plastic wrappers, basketballs, a wiener dog, and dozens of humans rapidly drained down the twenty-odd tubes, continuously replaced by roof hoppers on the rebound, bruised and frightened but ready for more.

Luis Manuel gazed suspiciously at the layer of foam in the water, grumbling something I couldn't understand.

"He wants to go to the highest launch," said Carlitos. "Faster tubes up there."

"Lead the way," I said.

Our bare feet made slurping sounds in the mud as we followed Luis Manuel a quarter mile to the highest pool. This one had a tenth the people, half the tubes, and five times more soldiers than the lower launch. I waded in and stroked for a tube, but—*Alto*! A young soldier would first have to take an official ride. "*Por qué*?" asked Luis Manuel.

"*El gordo. El gordísimo!*" said a private, knee-deep in

the murky water and clutching an old rifle. Someone prodigiously large had apparently just taken off, so he would first have to flush the tube, for our safety. Luis Manuel grabbed our arms and we kicked over to another tube and slipped in, me clutching Luis Manuel's ankles, and Carlitos, sheet-white and trembling, clinging on to mine. Logic said to go one at a time, but not in Venezuela, where anything worth doing is worth doing en masse. So we went all at once.

The turns were five-degree welded elbows, so at the first turn we were jolted apart, as were half of Luis Manuel's remaining teeth and most of my vertebrae. Heavy flow meant mossy tubes and, in seconds, we vaulted into blackness and slammed through another turn. *If I hit another bend, I'll dent the tube,* I thought, trying to ignore the screams of careening bodies. After a long minute and a few hundred yards, as my nuts had shrunk to chickpeas, light showed far ahead. We rifled out into free space, flailing to avoid hitting each other, and free-fell 25 feet into the turbid mud of the aqueduct.

We swam to shore, rubbing our barked hips and shoulders. Nobody could stop laughing and Carlitos carried on as though he'd just slain the Hydra with his bare hands. "It takes a set of *huevos* to take that ride, *primo*," he yelled. We kicked back in the mud and watched for a while. Better than half the tube-shooters were women and girls, but Carlitos kept on about his *huevos grandes*.

An 80-foot cement wall dammed the uphill end of the aqueduct, festooned with a dozen pissing tubes, whose positions varied from below the waterline to near the top of the wall. So far as I understood, the tubes were fed by nearby rivers and *lagunas*, and all of them emptied into the aqueduct, a fact that took several misadventures to establish. No one wanted to repeat the accidental feat of the Cariña boy, who got sucked into the inaugural ride, and verified where the tubes dumped out and that a body could survive the passage unscathed. But this was something that deserved double-, even triple-checking, so, according to Luis Manuel, a National Guardsmen got the wise idea to chuck stray dogs into the tubes and find out that way. The bit about feeding a black dog in one end and a white dog splashing down in the aqueduct—its coat blanched from fear—sounded like bullshit. But Luis Manuel promised all tubes were vetted and ridden many times. And the exit was the best thing about it.

From tubes high and low on the 80-foot wall, screaming bodies came whistling forth, backward, upside down, landing on friends who had landed on friends. Everyone howled as the human torpedoes, stunned and dumbfounded, hobbled over to the bank, collapsed into the mud, and licked their wounds.

"*¡Coooooooño!*" shrieked Luis Manuel. I caught sight of a girl, maybe 16, rocketing out at the 60-foot level. Her scream could have woken Simón Bolívar, and she pawed the air like a cat as everyone below dove for their lives. Whop! A 10-point bellyflop. But she quickly stroked to the bank and raced off.

"*Vamo, pue*," said Luis Manuel, jumping to his feet.

"The *gaffo* can't let a girl outdo us," Carlitos said to me, white and shaking again.

We scampered after the girl, but lost her in the crowd. Just to our right, steady traffic staggered to and from a cordoned area surrounded by a dozen menacing soldiers.

"Oh, that?" said Carlitos, encouraged we'd lost the girl. "Liquor is forbidden anywhere near the tubes. Much too dangerous. But anyone willing to join that huddle can drink themselves half dead and go right back to the pipes. You figure it out."

Back at the high mudhole, Luis Manuel spotted some footprints leading up through the muck to higher ground, and we tracked them to a small rivulet, vacant save for the girl we'd seen delivered high above the aqueduct. Luis Manuel beamed as the girl peered into three half-submerged tubes. "These babies look a little rusty," I said. Luis Manuel scoffed and, with a casual hand flick, said most of the pipes were old and repurposed to begin with. And it didn't matter anyhow because everyone knew all pipes led to *Roma*. Luis Manuel questioned the girl, who answered by slipping headfirst into the middle pipe.

"Oh, sheeeet," Carlitos said, as Luis Manuel waded over to the middle tube. "We best take this one feet-first, muchacho. Better to have your feet take those bends than your freakin' *cabeza*."

Sage advice, since soon after the entrance, the tube angled down sharply, slammed 'round a bend, and we shot into the darkness at speed. I tried to stay centered on the slime, clutching my gonads, praying I'd find no V-turns or sloppy welds. The girl's screams died off. The pipe vanished beneath me and I tumbled through the darkness 10 feet, 20—who knows how far—and I splashed into some sort of tank. No sound from the girl. I thrashed for Carlitos and we clasped hands and were whisked into a whirling eye like in a draining bathtub. We gasped what we reckoned were last breaths as the vortex sucked us down a thin, vertical shaft.

After the two longest seconds of my life we splashed into a pool, bounced off the bottom, and were gushed out into a larger pipe, recognizable by the more gentle curvature beneath our speeding gams. We pitched down a ramp so steep our arms flew up and we were racing all over again, slightly reassured by the stale air and Luis Manuel's distant screams. His shrieks shortly gave way to something sounding like a drumstick raked across a mile-long *charrasca*, a stuttering, wrenching racket we soon matched when we ground across a corrugated stretch that tweaked and pummeled every joint.

The aqueduct loomed miles behind us and, in total silence, we whistled along for an age, regaining some wits and a numbing terror. Finally, I managed a scream, as did Carlitos, somewhere behind. And Luis Manuel and the girl, both well ahead. We coursed through the darkness. My mind raced with images of the pipe forking into two, or getting extruded through a grate, or getting spit out the top of a 300-foot-high dam.

We bruised off a final bend and shot for a pinhole of

light. I breathed again, bashed across a final washboard, and only half-felt my 10-foot free-fall before landing into a pool of mushy green slime. I wobbled toward moving water to soak and check injuries. The girl had a strained neck and didn't know if she was dead or in Paraguay. Luis Manuel rubbed his collarbone as blood trickled from a gash on his chin. Carlitos hobbled around in circles, ranting about *huevos grandes* and some matador named Belmonte. The distant truck horns proclaimed the *autopista* a mile or so away. Hardly a great distance, but we'd have to hoof it naked since the tubes had stripped the suits off all four of us.

N
NW
NE
W
E
SW
ES
S

EL TIBURON

CARLITOS RETURNED FROM THE *LICORERÍA* with a case of Polar Lager, and we took our time loading the giant cooler and pouring three ice bags over the glistening brown bottles.

"You're thinking the ice cools down the beer," said Carlitos. "In fact, the ice sucks the heat from the bottles. It's called convection."

"You're making that shit up," I said.

"Give me the keys," said Marisol. Carlitos went to complain and she cut him off. "If you *payasos* are drinking your way across the *sabana*, I'm driving."

Carlitos handed Marisol the keys and we piled into the panel van, rolled out of El Tigre and across the *gran sabana*, heading for the coast. The sweet musk of mint thicket and *flor de Mayos* swirled in through the windows, left open to kill the heat. Back then, if you hankered for tropical exotica with a side order of beauty queens (I married one), *frijoles negros*, and fried plantains, you couldn't do better than Venezuela. But it takes some getting used to.

Life "down south" runs decidedly postmodern as it defies the tenets of structured narrative. You start something—rarely on time—but never arrive at the middle because you've already strayed toward anything that shines, amazes, smells good, has magical powers, is big and fancy, is fat, scary, complicated, tiny, very noble, or stinks to high heaven—all compelling reasons to jag sideways and discover where it takes you. And because little ever accrues, second acts go missing and endings are simply the moment you fall asleep. A new day comes, and a new beginning, and onward you go in random lurches. A person with a one-track mind can make a fortune down here, but she'll have few friends and no fun. This might better characterize myself than anyone in South America, but maybe you get the picture.

Marisol and my wife, Teresa, took turns driving and swerving around potholes three feet across and veering onto the dirt shoulder when the asphalt vanished or a mattress blocked the way. Every six years a new governor promised to fix the roads. No one knew where the money went but it never made it onto the highway, which stretched off arrow-straight across vast pastureland veined by lazy streams, all blues and greens heaped upon an unbroken horizon. Far in the distance, a lone horseman led a few cattle. The cowboy could walk for days, but there'll always be more *sabana*. Always the *sabana*.

"Can a man get some music back here?" asked Carlitos.

The old tape player, lashed to the dash with wire and duct tape, cannibalized everything from *Gaita* harp music to proto-merengue tunes with enough horn play to raise the dead. The one cassette to survive came courtesy of 1950s era balladeer, Julio Jaramillo, whose heart was so broken we couldn't stand it. So we sang along. It was Christmas Eve. None of us had religion, but the yuletide in Venezuela—synonymous with Catholic voodoo, food to die for, and a regular downpour of booze—is found money. And we meant to spend it all.

Marisol pulled into the long queue at the Conferry docks in Puerto La Cruz, where an armada of giant blue ferries looped to and from Isla Margarita, the "Pearl of the Caribbean." Teresa's extended family was largely *Margariteños* who had moved off the island but still had homes there, or had relatives with homes and who'd always return for the holidays. We'd head over for Christmas and New Years and continued this tradition till my two daughters left for college.

Around midnight we joined the crowd rolling onto the ferry, climbing a steep metal staircase above the *motos*, jalopies, and big rigs overflowing with trade goods and stowed below. Hundreds of passengers swarmed the upper decks. We walled off a little square with the cooler and the twenty bags we'd lugged on board, laying out thin foam pads for dozing. In minutes the entire deck, long and wide as a soccer pitch, resembled an emergency shelter during hurricane season, with laughing heads jutting from swaying hammocks strung off poles and port hole hinges, water boiling on small camp stoves while hands snatched cakes, liter bottles of Pepsi-Cola, *empanadas*, and colorful fruits off cloths spread over the deck. Jokes were cracked, mosquitos were swatted as kids tossed balls and frisbees. The *Mundana* from Caracas let her lap dog roam and it peed on the purser's cowboy boots. Meanwhile, somebody's great-great-aunt sat in a deck chair reciting the Rosary, her crooked brown fingers moving the beads on the string, as the ferry chugged towards open water. The commotion slowly settled, the lights were dimmed, and the moment the women and children lay down, Carlitos said, "*Vamanos*," and we joined the men crowding the open space near the prow, talking shit and watching the stars.

"It's forty-nine miles to Margarita," said Carlitos, "but the ferries are old and one like this capsized in Somalia a few years ago and killed six hundred people."

Carlitos loved embroidering the facts. But no one could bolster this night, drinking *tragitos* of rum chased by ice-cold *cerveza* on board the MS Rosa Eugenia, which managed the trip across the water in less than five hours, landing at *Punta de Piedras* just as the sun came up.

Thick ropes looped down from masts high on the ferry and stretched over to great rusty thwarts on the docks. Skinny kids walked the steep ropes bare-footed and dove like thunderbolts after coins we threw into the water, sometimes 50 feet below. Many tried tricking the kids, throwing nuts and bolts and shiny whatevers they had scavenged off the ferry. But the kids only dived for real money.

"Couldn't tell you how they know the difference," said Carlitos, "but they always do."

We took a taxi to the shambling hacienda of Teresa's childhood friend, Luz, a Margarita native who had moved to Valencia after college. Her folks, Don Julio and Doña Rosalva, a retired schoolteacher, rarely left the island and had the two-story place in La Asunción, several blocks from the oldest church in Venezuela. Don Julio, also retired, had played valve trombone in the state orchestra and local salsa groups. Don Julio's son, Chico, drove a bus and drank the powerful local *caña* like water.

Margarita was renowned for accomplished drinkers.

Locals had appropriately rechristened then Governor Fucho Tovar (Fucho = diminutive for Rafael), *Mucho Tomar*, or big drinker. That's how people rolled before the Venezuelan currency tanked a decade later, when populist president Hugo Chavez ("*El Eterno*") and his Castro-inspired *socialismo* ran the country into the shitter and bankers and professors had to kill their pets for food. But the bolivar held strong for the moment so, for this trip and many that followed, we drank.

A big open square in the middle of the hacienda had the roof cut away. Afternoon showers fell in a torrent, filling plastic paint buckets, old tires, and other makeshift flowerpots overflowing with hibiscus and oleander. In that redolent pause after the rain stopped, moths and butterflies swarmed the blooms as a deep blue *mariposa* floated flower to flower like a piece of living sky. Magdalena del Valle Marcano-Reyes, Luz's great-grandmother, sat in unhinged majesty, propped in a plastic lawn chair pulled back clear of the rain.

"She's well over a hundred years old," said Carlitos, as we paid our regards to Grandmama, wrapped in a saffron robe and sitting regally in the front room space, a newspaper spread beneath her chair to check periodic discharges.

Brother Chico lounged in a hammock, watching English League *fútbol* on a black-and-white TV and working a liter of Old Parr. Margarita was a duty-free island so quality booze came cheap, a discount that killed more locals than old age, heart disease, and cancer combined. Chico used the bottle cap as a shot glass—a chintzy way to drink,

I thought—except he'd tilt the bottle at commercial breaks, so he drained it quickly enough. Once we got the kids settled, we drove over to visit Kin Ting—that's the phonetic spelling, and I've no idea where the Siamese-sounding name came from since the man was Creole head to toe. Don Julio had known Kin Ting since grade school, going back seventy years.

Margarita describes an hourglass on its side. Most residents live on the more developed eastern half of the island, near the duty-free shopping in Porlamar, a favorite getaway for Dutch, Swiss, and German tourists fleeing fierce Euro winters. Kin Ting lived and fished on the western, leeward coast, where he and Don Julio were born. The single lane road passed through a narrow isthmus and slashed through jade hedgerow climbing right to a ridge, while plunging left straight into the ocean. Clouds skittered over the working sea, where turquoise winked to blue, silver, slate, and aquamarine.

"Agnostics never make it this far," said Carlitos, repeating the local phrase. "But Christopher Columbus did." The green mountain, said Carlitos, an albino mermaid, and other miraculous sightings fleshed out Christopher's journal, which he presented to Spain's King Ferdinand in 1492. Carlitos talked freely with curious facts and I doubted them all.

Just past El Manglillo, "which has more dogs then people," according to locals, we followed a dirt road to rolling sand drifts and terraced rock. Old builders had cobbled a few dozen cinderblock houses into stony hollows, reminiscent of the Anasazi dwellings at Mesa Verde. A tin-roofed A-frame, set back from the sea, covered a massif of nylon nets. We met Kin Ting, climbed onto his motorized skiff, and headed out over flat water.

Kin Ting, burned black as a tire, had the far-reaching gaze you sometimes find in cowboys and Bedouins who live in open spaces. He stayed in the prow, mostly, stoically pointing directions to his grandson, Felipe, who manned the tiller with both hands and whose eyes never left his grandfather. Felipe wore his new Christmas trunks and a baseball cap for his favorite team, the Caracas Lions. The fishermen had the day off, but their lives belonged to the sea.

Only a certain kind of person, who fits in awkwardly most everywhere else, finds sanctuary on the big water. The ocean keeps them poor and exhausted, and gets chancy when the trade winds blow, so rational people don't normally work there. But they rarely have what the fisherman has: magic. Adrift in old rhythms. And drinking whiskey when they feel like it. Kin Ting had a fifth of Glenlivet and he'd frequently pass the bottle around the horn. Then we'd motor on to no place in particular, never dreaming of being somewhere else. I'd been awake for days so, next time we paused, I dove into the water to clear the cobwebs. Currents I never saw swept me off toward Trinidad. I dog-paddled like mad but drifted farther to sea until Kin Ting motored over and hauled me in with a calloused paw.

"Forget about swimming in these waters," I said.

"You'd be right about that," said Kin Ting. "But *El*

Tiburón—"

Don Julio stirred at mention of that name, which means shark in Spanish. *El Tiburón* remained a legend with local fishermen and, like everyone on this side of the island, Carlitos had suffered the stories so many times he could scream. Then he'd repeat them ad nauseum. Now, *El Tiburón*'s name was heard less and less because he was going on 80 and had hung up his nets years before, though he still swam for exercise. And far, said Kin Ting. In the days before motors, Kin Ting and friends would row the nets out to set their buoys. No one remembers when, but *El Tiburón* began swimming out the nets with a rope lashed 'round his waist. He could drag the nets for miles, sometimes towing the boats behind him, sometimes with a knife between his teeth—surely a poetic touch—and occasionally getting separated from the flotilla and having to swim ashore from way out there. One time, *El Tiburón* got snagged by evil currents that hauled him halfway to Curaçao, and his family feared him dead till, a day later, he washed ashore in Paraguachí, miles down the coast.

Glenlivet did the talking, but Don Julio and Kin Ting kept nodding their heads, saying, "*Es verdad*," as Carlitos related the old stories he grew up with, and which we immediately forgot as we drove back across the isthmus.

Chico was roundly drunk. And worried. "Officials," which mean many things in Venezuela, had selected him to help carry the Virgin. Virgins are accorded extraordinary powers all across the Caribbean, and I wondered which one Chico had been chosen to carry, and to where. Whatever. Chico had to get to The Sanctuary, over in Margarita Valley, right now. Don Julio reminded us nothing during Christmas season ever came off on time, so relax. I still worked slightly in the dark per Venezuela, having only been married five years.

Cars, parked bumper-to-bumper, lined the streets surrounding The Sanctuary, a white shrine for *La Virgin del Valle*, Virgin of the Valley and patroness of eastern Venezuela. A life-sized effigy of the child Virgin, with a pearl-encrusted cape and solid gold tiara, garlanded with white roses, was bolted to a wooden platform big as a billiard table. Red velvet curtains draped over a dozen bearers hunkered underneath the platform, who shouldered the Virgin around the mob. Only someone born into old-school Margarita could feel the beating heart of this sacrament, clearly a great event. Aside from a few thousand pilgrims, a group of dignitaries—mostly priests and Venezuelan naval officers—turned out in garish ceremonial outfits, sat, and sweated on a stage. The ritual borrowed from the Hajj, where mobs of Muslim faithful circle the sacred Kaaba stone. Except here, they paraded the Virgin around the dignitaries, who rose as She passed, crossing themselves and drawing sabers and saluting while, off to one side, a girl in fashionably ripped jeans, heels, and mirrored sunglasses butchered "Ave Maria" on a megaphone.

The problem was liquor. And heat. Especially in the cloistered space under the Virgin's platform, where Chico stooped and shouldered and marched with friends. They'd all done little but drink through the whole vacation. Fresh air could scarcely penetrate the velvet curtains. After several laps around The Sanctuary, the Virgin herself looked loopy as Her platform rocked and pitched. Then, one poor bearer upchucked, fomenting a cruel miasma that had no escape and triggered a chain reaction. The holy procession survived only because the mob grabbed the platform at the last second, before it went over and The Virgin took a dive.

For one suspended moment the whole raucous, high-blown, holy-watered production tumbled into farce. Who was this Virgin but the kitschy custodian of chastity for every Juanita in eastern Venezuela? Or the bishops and generals swaggering on stage, a fêted band of *fanfarróns* play-acting in Halloween costumes. And all the adorable little girls in their colorful party dresses and shiny shoes and braided hair, their tiny lips painted red. As if their hovering mothers sought to sugar and preserve them like fruit. Or like the child Virgin Herself—that the girls should never age and do the naughty with us fuckoffs and *borrachos*, and never learn every heart is broken and we all must die. Who wouldn't grope after God? And when God went missing we drank a little more. The drinking that made corpses. And the girl with the megaphone sang a little louder. Anything to ease the death of miracles.

The rest of that visit is a blur. The booze and fatigue and New Year's chaos spun me into a wormhole I couldn't escape till leaving Margarita a week later and flying back to L.A.

The following Christmas, I found myself back in the house in La Asunción, watching rain fall through the hole in the roof as Chico, parked in his hammock, worked a bottle in the corner. In order to control our own drinking, Carlitos and I swore off daylight boozing and spent the time running, hiking, hitting the gym, and playing pick-up basketball. And we ate smart, too. No greasy fried crap. Only fruit, vegetables, and lean meats. Through this routine, we spent the greater part of our day boosting health and sanity, which we believed limited the carnage when the sun set and we started drinking like crazy.

During an afternoon jog by Playa Varadero, we noticed several trucks emblazoned with logos for *Cervecería Nacional*, a popular Venezuelan beer. Twenty day-hires and their boss, a Benicio del Toro look-alike in purple board shorts, worked like beavers erecting bleachers on the sand and inflating an arch serving as the finish and starting line for an open-ocean swimming race. Benicio said triathletes and watermen had arrived from all over to compete. An Olympic hopeful from the national team was favored to win, but local money was on a Cuban named Rubio. Benicio grinned as he told us Governor Fucho Tovar would personally supervise the bikini contest. A big motor launch had dropped anchor a mile-and-a-half offshore—the turnaround point for the out-and-back swim—and a tethered *Nacional* blimp hovered above it. *Nacional* had donated fifty kegs of pilsner beer, so twenty-five kegs might get there.

"So long as the beer lasts," said Carlitos, "Mucho Tomar will hang around and so will the crowd. This could be legendary."

Helpers offloaded a long surf ski (a sit-on-top kayak) from the *Nacional* truck. Benicio said, as a promotional gimmick, they'd scheduled a local waterman named *El Tiburón* to perform a short demonstration swim before the official race kicked off. The surf ski would follow the ancient fisherman in case he tired and needed a little something to hang onto. I reminded Carlitos about the yarns he'd recited about *El Tiburón* during our expedition on Kin Ting's boat—how The Shark swam nets out with a knife between his teeth and treaded water all night long in a hurricane.

"And was born in the ocean to a mermaid," said Carlitos, and how he later washed ashore in Trinidad, clinging to a snapping turtle, something even Don Julio thought unlikely. And now this Creole Poseidon would swim a few strokes for the crowd, who knew him from the classic stories, or not at all.

Back at the house in La Asunción, a handful of retired fishermen, all grade school pals of Don Julio's, had joined us to eat glistening loaves of *pan de jamón* (a smashing sweet bread-and-ham medley) and the traditional Christmas *hallaca*—marinated pork, raisins, capers, and olives wrapped in cornmeal dough, swaddled with plantain leaves, tied with twine, and boiled like a tamale. Interlarded with strategic shots of rum and a tidal drift of cold lager, the yuletide carried us far. The women drank sweet Uruguayan wine and sang carols, and we men moved into the front room to play checkers.

Someone produced a bottle of *Cacique*, a local rum, which drains straight to the migraine crook in your brainpan and sloshes around for days. Carlitos put on some Dominican salsa music and mentioned their *paisano, El Tiburón*, would perform his demo swim at the comp the next afternoon. They must be excited to have their fellow fisherman representing at such a big event, he added. The fishermen never glanced up from the checkerboard. I mentioned the rescue kayak, in case *El Tiburón* tired, and they chuckled. Carlitos thought it reckless to have an old man out there battling those currents, kayak or not.

Finally, one fisherman spoke. *El Tiburón* always attended afternoon mass, he said, since he retired years ago. So why would he screw around with spoiled brats swimming in his ocean? If *El Tiburón* showed up at all, he'd swim the same race as everyone else. And he'll win going away. The others grumbled, "*Claro*," and "*Por seguro*," and moved the red-and-black pieces around the boards.

"*Por favor*," said Carlitos. As if some waterlogged grouper, pushing 80 years old, could keep pace with Olympic-caliber distance swimmers and triathletes. I waved a hand at Carlitos—it wouldn't do to mock retired old fishermen who knew less about modern athletes than thermodynamics. One fisherman, built like a rhino, thrust the *Cacique* bottle at me and said, "Go over to Playa Varadero tomorrow. If *El Tiburón* shows up, you'll see for yourselves." The others said nothing, suffering us as fools, which felt quaint and wonderful.

Next afternoon, Carlitos and I jogged over to Playa Varadero and watched the crowd gather while a rock band from Puerto la Cruz threatened to blow out the sun. *Nacional* held good to their word about the fifty kegs. A dozen hostesses trimmed out in blue satin *Nacional* bikini tops brimmed tankards of beer quick as we shoved them under the tap. An athletes-only area near the start, below the inflatable *Nacional* arch, filled with swimmers small-talking and psyching each other. With *Nacional* giving real money to the first ten finishers, these guys meant business. Several females also came to race, including a pale-skinned giantess named Prima Doña, with close-cropped, bleach blonde hair and a wire-thin, creeping vine tattoo winding around her torso. We couldn't take our eyes off her. Rubio, the Cuban favorite, resembled a deep-fried James Dean. Even had the pout. With all this going on we hardly noticed the old man pushing a rusty bike across the sand.

"That's gotta be him," said Carlitos, elbowing me in the ribs. *El Tiburón*, taller than I'd imagined, and more golden than brown, had barnyard shoulders and a Saint Anthony face as rucked and seamed as the floor of Lago Maracaibo. He set his bike against the arch, padlocked it, walked over to a portable spray unit, and stood in the misty curtain like a triton in a fountain, staring out to sea. As the fisherman had promised, *El Tiburón* came to race, something so incidental to the proper competition it barely earned mention over the loudspeaker.

We stood outside the roped-off area and had a clear view of the other athletes, who hardly noticed and didn't care about the wrinkly fisherman swimming in their contest. Three minutes and counting. The competitors stripped to trunks and windmilled their arms, jostling for position at the starting line, a short ways inland from the *Nacional* arch. The crowd tightened at the edges. We elbowed around in order to keep staring at Prima Doña's granite corpus. *El Tiburón* stood motionless at the rear of the pack.

"*Cuatro, tres, dos, uno—*"

The gun sounded and the swimmers stormed across the sand and dove into the sea, surfacing in a flurry, their arms thrashing the water. All but *El Tiburón*, who walked toward the water on unsteady pins. To his right, a young man dragged the rescue surf ski, just in case. The main pack had built a sizable lead as El Tiburón duck-dove under the shorebreak and pulled his first stroke, which brought a charity roar from the crowd. The kayaker flipped in the surf but quickly crawled back aboard and stroked after *El Tiburón*. Carlitos and I grabbed a beer and trudged up to a bluff overlook, where the bikini models preened, signed hats and t-shirts, and slapped a hundred traveling hands.

Out at sea, the pack quickly lengthened into a loose chain, churning past small breakers in the shallows and clearing a sea ledge where the ocean floor dropped off and the water went gray to deep blue. In open ocean at last, swirling currents yanked the chain apart, sending the pack in all directions, as a stain spreads out on a blue tablecloth. An on-shore wind and oblique rolling swells doubled their trouble. Even the lead swimmers only could pull a few clean strokes before the rip broke their rhythm and pulled them sideways. The stronger swimmers held a ragged trajectory, but they covered 15 or 20 feet to gain 10 on the motor launch and the turnaround, still better than a mile out there.

El Tiburón, far behind, swam at a casual but fluid clip. But once he pulled into open water, he looked little affected by the violent riptides, gliding through hidden troughs. Now he hitchhiked onto the off-shore edge of whorls, thrusting him out at speed, as if he and the currents were on speaking terms. Slowly, he closed the distance with the stragglers in the main pack.

"Old fart might make that boat out there," said Carlitos. The kayaker tired of fighting the currents and turned around. If *El Tiburón* couldn't gain the motor launch, we'd have a dead fisherman on our hands. The swimmers shrank to specks, waning to occasional white flashes, till only a working sea stretched vacantly out to the motor launch and the tethered *Nacional* blimp, two dots bobbing on the blue horizon. Time for another beer.

The crowd defied gravity and flowed uphill to the bluff overlook, where the bikini girls staged a bump-and-grind dancing comp on a flatbed truck as the band played at 100 decibels. A trophy and two judges in matching *guayaberas* lent the contest a veneer of respectability. Then the generator conked out and we stood there, waiting for the swimmers to stroke back into view.

I headed over to the hot dog cart—and ran into Governor Rafael "Fucho" Tovar. Though I grew up with Spanish, locals always know I speak "the English," and Fucho's wasn't half bad. He'd learned by listening to Frank Sinatra LPs and watching *I Love Lucy*, he said. We both bought dogs and Fucho garnished his handsomely with mustard, onions, mayo, and croutons. I mentioned Prima Doña—not that the governor would have noticed—and I thought the man might weep. Whatever else one might say about Fucho Tovar, he stood right there with the rest of us common Jose's, sans bodyguard and fanfare, the gazillionaire owner of Conferry, who once sold empanadas off a dog cart in front of his house in nearby Juan Griego, who later left for Caracas and worked in banking, went to law school, fought his way into the Senate, the governor's office, then dropped by the swimming comp there at Playa Varadero and bought himself a dog. I stood little chance of sharing a frank with such a man in an American or European country. And this wholesale disregard for hierarchy—even while they lie, steal, and kill for the upper rungs—gives Latin America, for all of its blunders and *basura*, a special place in human culture.

"Holy shit," said Carlitos, glassing the open ocean with binos he'd begged off a Dutch tourist. The swimmers kept growing on the horizon and we moved in a crush to the edge of the bluff, where a bikini girl tripped and took a nasty tumble to the sand below, and where fifty wandering hands maneuvered her back to her feet. Carlitos passed me the binos and I framed the first three swimmers, roughly moving together, several hundred yards in front of the others. *El Tiburón* was one of the leaders. The Dutch tourist snatched back his binos and Carlitos and I scrambled down to the beach.

Word quickly spread, "*El Tiburón*" repeated a thousand times in thirty seconds. The great fisherman was pushed by unseen hands; only a fellow *Margariteño* could swim so wonderfully and, according to the man yammering over the loudspeaker, we were witnessing a *milagro*—a miracle. *El Tiburón* could never keep pace with the other two in an Olympic pool. But traversing open ocean across the squirrely-watered, windward side of the island, *El Tiburón* was nonpareil, less swimming than navigating the rips and whorls.

The other two leaders—Rubio the Cuban, and Prima Doña—struggled to track the duffer's course. Lacking his feel for the currents, they tried to compensate with furious strokes. Slowly, they tired and fell back as *El Tiburón*, with the wind and swells behind him, squirted over the sea ledge, snagged a gentle comber, and bodysurfed onto the sand. Police and lifeguards fought off cameramen and the converging mob, giving El Tiburón a clear path to the beach, through the inflatable *Nacional* arch and the finish line. But *El Tiburón* hadn't run in twenty years, so he shuffled toward the arch in no kind of hurry as Rubio and Prima Doña closed behind him. The crowd jumped and shouted "¡*Ándale*!" and "¡*Ir*!" as if their pleas might blow the old man to victory. Instead, we all watched *El Tiburón* stop like a boss and rinse himself off in the sprayer as Rubio and the giantess sprinted past.

Attention swung to the finish line, where Prima Doña out-leaned the Cuban by a nose. The mob crushed in and paraded Prima Doña around—ten boys at each elbow—as the band played "Tush" on the bluff. Carlitos and I jostled over to the arch, but *El Tiburón* had already left.

"Probably to Mass," said Carlitos.

N
W
E
S

FREJA

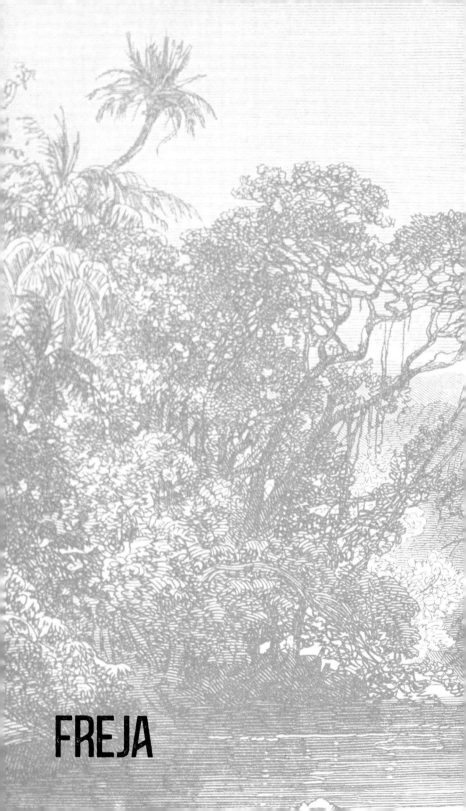

DIEGO WORKED AS A TOUR GUIDE who took foreigners on simple nature hikes on the Island of Margarita. He worked for Hilton Hotels and his morning strolls along the beach and through nearby jungle were favorites among wealthy Europeans. They flew over in droves during Christmas break, when in Stockholm and Zurich the snow stood barn-high and the föhn wind howled. One morning I shagged along with Diego when he took a group of Danish tourists on walkabout.

The Danes numbered a dozen, few younger than 50, respectful to a fault, civil but chilly, and asked more questions than an 8-year-old. Except Freja. She didn't say a word. Like the others, she'd overdressed for the tropics, with her crepe silk slacks and linen blouse. She'd spun her graying blond hair into a glossy bun the size of an acorn. Her carriage was painfully regal, her face attractive but blank, and she didn't so much walk as march, stiffly, across the beach sand and into leafy jungle, as though attending a coronation. Or a funeral.

The others kept asking Diego about the narrow footpath, the spiraling vines, the squawking birds, though I'm guessing, since they kept switching between English and German. Diego's father was Venezuelan, his mother, British, and he'd just completed a computer science degree from the Berlin Institute of Technology. The Danes, who treasure education, admired his language skills.

A quarter mile into the jungle we found a wide, flat clearing floored with spongy turf, like an overgrown putting green. The Danes stamped curiously on the turf, and retired in twos to a bubbling spring close by. Except Freja, apparently single, who stood like a statue on the edge of the grass. Diego, an accomplished card shark and reggaeton drummer, had a knack for discovering people's leg irons and, right on the spot, reckoning a means of escape. Most clients were one-and-done, unlikely to ever take another tour, or to experience jungle again, so he had one shot to leave clients with some freedom.

I was rummaging in my pack when Diego coaxed a few words from Freja. She relaxed a notch, and they continued talking. When Diego asked her an apparently probing question, she smirked and glanced at me. I smiled. Freja shrugged a shoulder, kicked off her shoes, and slowly walked out across the spongy turf. Tentatively at first, her toes probing the green stuff. Diego said to keep walking (I think) and, with each step, I watched the brittle tension drain from her body, till she paused in the middle, with her arms slightly outstretched and her palms turned up. She smiled at the sky as she turned in a slow circle.

The others returned from the spring; Freja slipped her shoes back on and, as Diego led the group back to the pool at the Hilton, Freja's face once again went blank as she walked back into her regal carriage.

Later, answering my burning question, Diego said he'd asked Freja how she might walk if nobody was watching. She'd glanced at me because I *was* watching, but the question felt too inviting. So she kicked off her shoes and broke out into the open. Of course, we never saw her again, and I imagine she went back to Aalborg or Odense, taut, blank, and majestic as she'd arrived in Margarita. But she'd always have her moment on the green turf, when Freja from Denmark climbed off her throne and walked among the living.

FATHER JAVY

VALENCIA, VENEZUELA sits in a central valley bordered to the north by a coastal ridge of jutting peaks. I spent much of the year in Valencia, after getting married to a Venezuelan schoolteacher I met during a film shoot at Angel Falls. I still kept a small place in Los Angeles, and often returned there for work. But I'd bought a house and had two kids in Venezuela, so Valencia was home. And home was a torture chamber.

Most afternoons, my wife would dump me and our corroding marriage at the base of the cordillera, and I'd trudge the ancient trail snaking up to the ridgeline. That's where I first met Father "Javy" (short for Javier), a former national middle-distance runner, and a Jesuit who never drank. I usually hiked with a hangover, sometimes a rager, and the ground would rock and spin. Father Javy taught psychology at Universidad de Carabobo, there in town, and worked in public psych wards—which often doubled as jails. He loved art. During one of our evening hikes he mentioned gathering works for a new museum at El Club, a local private resort. The museum targeted homegrown artists, said the Father, though the first exhibit, opening in a week, would feature works by Stella, Chagall, Kline, and others.

"You forgot Kandinsky," I said. "And doesn't Saint Geronimo's have a splinter from Jesus' cross?" The Father grinned. Valencia had dozens of parishes, including Geronimo's.

"You'll be there to help me at the opening, of course," said the Father, who had fancy degrees from Villanova and Notre Dame. "And I'll watch you eat those words."

Better than eating his dust. I lived in a kind of Chernobyl-of-the-soul after years of toxic meltdowns with my wife. And all those bottles. Father Javy faced his own torments, rarely mentioned. We both took it out on the trail. Only through mutual exhaustion did we ever come clean with each other. Most evenings we'd hunt those moments all along the ridgeline, chasing the sun as it flared on the horizon like a struck match.

The gallery's soft opening included local media and a handful of VIPs. Valencia is Venezuela's industrial and financial hub, and generates much of the country's wealth, so a whole lot of El Club members had a whole lot of money—never mind how they got it. They'd sunk a fortune into the elegant, flagstone structure they'd built out for the new museum. A club official cut the ribbon and Father Javy led us though the chain of rectangular rooms with hardwood floors and matte-white walls. Ceiling-mounted track lights cast a noir atmosphere on the fifty mostly abstract paintings.

Father Javy had filled the first two gallery spaces with original works by Venezuelan artists (borrowed from national museums), long on light spears and colored shrapnel. Room three went global, first with Helen Frankenthaler's *Mountains and Sea*. It felt like I could curl up and sleep it off in the jutting smears of blue and green on Helen's canvas. Evocative work, though it hardly outshined local efforts. But Art Market Monitor had recently valued the Frankenthaler at 15 million dollars, according to Estela Fontana, a young op-ed columnist for *El Carabobeño*. We were standing several paces back from the painting which, at first blush, looked so genuine I thought a local *millonario* had bought the original and loaned it to the Father for the opening.

"You figured I'd slap up a couple prints from the MoMA design store," the Father chuckled when he saw me eying Stella's *Virgin of the Rose and Lily*, highly prized by the mostly Catholic crowd. "Just saying," I said as we floated on, borne aloft, or so it seemed, by several billion dollars-worth of art. The designer had modeled the room after the temp exhibit wing in the Guggenheim, and just wandering through I felt like a bit player in a James Bond film. Pollock's *Mural*, all 20 by 8 feet of it, took an entire wall of the final chamber. It gave off its own force field.

I shot the Father a "What the hell?" look. He smiled and confided to Estela and I that none of the European or American works were original, rather "authentic replicas." Estela laughed at the term and asked what made them authentic. "Their likeness to the originals," said the Father, who'd given high-res digital files to club member Ulises Montenegro, a local with a printing company that fashioned giclee panels of the works on flannel nap linen paper. So skillfully had they stitched the panels together that, from a few steps back, a knock-off of Paul Klee's *View from Red*, and others, were indistinguishable from the originals.

Father Javy had gone with works that moved his dial and hauled him outside his comfort zone. Not all of those present were so progressive, and some sneered at the abstracts as they might a crossdresser. But this was the grand opening, so anyone feeling scandalized stayed quiet.

The tour ended at *El Salón de Bolívar*, a smaller gallery space attached to the main structure, built to house a given exhibit's master work. *El Sueño de Rumulos*, in this case, an opulent fake of a giltwood-and-plaster frame, with a blank canvas inside. With conceptual offerings like this, your mileage will vary by what kind of art snob you are. But Rumulos's *Dream* was another swipe at a minimalist con pulled many times in many places, so who cared? Father Javy. Less, I had the feeling, about a blank canvas and a phony gold frame, and more where the stunt might lead us. It led most of the crowd straight out the front door and over to *La Gran Rotonda* for eight cases of Peruvian Sauvignon Blanc and a tray of tiny weenies on toothpicks. Father Javy stayed behind with Estela Fontana, and their conversation must have been a good one by the way the two kept laughing.

The next afternoon, Estela Fontana reported Rumulos's *Dream* had been stolen from El Club's museum. Father Javy provided photographs, which deepened the intrigue. The media piled on, each source offering slightly different accounts of an increasingly daffy narrative. I closely followed these accounts, which distracted me from the quagmire in my home front. After a week, Father Javy called a news conference to clarify *The Dream*'s tribulations.

The club's board of directors, the media, and I all crammed into *El Salón de Bolívar.* A scarlet sheet covered the back wall of the museum. Father Javy told us how a thief had stolen *The Dream* and swapped it out with a similar frame and blank canvas purchased at Pepina's Art

Depot, a local wholesaler. Club security officers collared the thief—the club's tennis pro—and recovered the purloined *Dream* at the pro's casa in Aguas Termales, a few miles away, and returned it to the museum for physical examination. The Father couldn't hide his embarrassment that the two frames got mixed up during analysis. Since the original and the replacement sported the same model frame and canvas, he went on, made by the same Chinese manufacturer, both purchased from Pepina's Art Depot, he could no longer discern the *camelo* (baloney in English, to use Estela Fontana's term) from the legitimate *Dream*. And without some means of authentication, he'd decided to decommission both "works" till they could unravel the mystery.

Father Javy had the deft pap of a charlatan, which he wasn't. Nevertheless, the blank canvas gag couldn't be older news. So the crowd encouraged Father Javy to save it and yank the saffron sheet off whatever the hell it covered on the rear wall of *El Salón*, where Rumulos once dreamt. Father Javy obliged, and the crowd looked unimpressed to see the same imitation Louis XV-style giltwood-and-plaster frame from Pepina's.

"Not at all," said Father Julio, already two steps ahead. "Look closer, *damas y caballeros*. Sculptress Palmira de la Vega calls it, *Espacio Puro*."

A Globovision reporter stepped close to the faux-gold frame, tapping a thin glass pane that had replaced the blank canvass, the bare wall visible behind it. Twenty-five *por favors* rang from the crowd. "¡*No hay nada ahí*!" somebody yelled. Nothing there at all.

"Yes, and no," said the Father. "We seem to live in a world of solid objects..."

Palmira de la Vega sounded like a stage name if ever we'd heard one. A twice-enacted gag is just dumb. The crowd was over Father Javy. People spilled into the preceding chamber, pausing at Pollock's *Mural*, snarling from the wall. People were too polite to have ripped on the Pollock during the grand opening, but this second time through, a handful snarled back.

"My daughter could paint that," said Francisco Ruiz-Cepeda, who owned a German degree in engineering, a shipping company, and a large swath of Valencia.

"Would you care to place a wager on that?" said Father Javy.

"*Lo que sea*," said Estela Fontana.

"Prove to anyone that *basura* is art," said another, rather funning the Father.

"With your kind assistance, we can do so," said Father Javy.

"How might I be of service?" said Francisco. Nobody wanted to appear the rube, but others immediately chimed in, eager to call the Father a trickster and proclaim their own virtue.

"If your daughter can do this," said Father Javy, motioning toward the Pollock, "you can too." The Saturday after next, the Father explained, they would stage an Art Day in The Great Rotunda. They'd invite the press and selected dignitaries, and all would test their hand at fashioning abstract art. "Unless you're afraid to try."

More *por favors* and chuckles. Who's afraid of a little paint? Father Javy had that little grin of his. Nothing was exactly as it seemed. It only took him a few minutes and he'd recruited many of those required for his demonstration. The crowd broke up, leaving Francisco Ruiz-Cepeda, Estela Fontana, and the Father, chuckling by the *araguaney* tree.

"Estela Fontana and Francisco Ruiz are ringers," I told the Father as we jogged the ridge that evening. "You knew people would pot-shot Jackson Pollock. Hell, yahoos do the same at the Chrysler Museum. All your crapola about that stupid *Dream* was a ploy to stage your Art Day."

"None of that makes you smart," said the Father.

"Why not just announce it, and skip the rigmarole?"

"A challenge works best to arouse the *gente,*" he said. "Then people start talking their *paja*, and we watch the stadium fill."

News articles about Art Day appeared the next day in *El Carabobeño* and *Notitarde*, as well as on local talk shows. Media people knew trying to gauge abstract fare using the rubrics of representational art was like dancing about agriculture, and makes morons out of dilettantes like myself. We might know all the names and popular works, and talk a clever game, but few of us truly *get* these paintings. The press also knew Father Javy was all but begging for idiotic reactions, so they broke out the lampoon for the fun of it. Miguel Thorn, from *The Daily Journal,* suggested the Father jumpstart Art Day with a séance, like

Swedish kook and modern artist Hilma af Klint did, back in the 1920s. Klint wouldn't approach her easel till she'd hailed the "ancient masters." An online cartoon featured Father Javy with a clerical collar (he never wore one) and a wizard's hat, waving a wand over a surrealist sculpture.

After a week, Father Javy had enrolled all the archetypal characters who legitimatize events in Venezuela. The whole coterie would converge on Art Day the following Saturday. The press kept running the event up the flagpole, like before. Mix in Father Javy's penchant for speaking and writing with a Jesuit's smarts and formality, and Art Day was ritualized with almost religious unction, which cast a non-event into the lights. But I started feeling restless in the glare.

The Father's family owned a cement production plant in Barquisimeto, so an original part of him was native to the millionaires' club. I felt like an illegal immigrant who had little place or purpose at El Club, and none at all at home, where my wife and I kept battling in emotional blood sport. My father, a conservative family doctor, had warned me about marrying a woman from another race and culture. He had it all wrong. *Mi amor* and I were a big blue kite and we'd loft above the mountain tops. But the string broke and the ground came rushing up. I didn't want to die, but more than a few times I wished my wife would just dry up and blow away. There were many things long lost on me just starting to be known, and I rarely saw myself so clearly when, during one of our marathon hikes, I spewed all this at Father Javy.

"Let's get off this ridge and go to the club," he said.

The club. Tens of thousands were starving in Venezuela while I sought escape through high art and the high life at El Club. Then I'd return home and get crushed again, and return the favor to my wife. And start drinking. I never signed on to act so wrong and feel this twisted. I slumped onto the trail.

My oldest daughter was a first-year medical student and, after class that day, she said *Mamá* showed clear signs of late-onset mental illness. She refused help and gaslighted me down to the bone; I bit right back, trying to force a solution. And around and around we'd go. My daughter couldn't watch it any longer. Maybe I should consider what she'd done the year before: moving out. Returning to my dingy little place in Santa Monica, California, and leaving the wife alone. I'd gone all-in here—kids, friends, houses, cars, and memories, and all the stuff to prove it. Now, my very daughter was showing me the door.

"We're going," said Father Javy, who pulled me back to my feet.

The Father ordered some food from the club grill and we ate on tray tables inside the museum, where the Father spent occasional evenings alone "to consolidate." He had positioned on a chair, a few feet away, a cheap poster print of Turner's *Snow Storm*, all sea-motion, mist and light, enclosing the ghostly contours of a 19th-century steam ship.

"Turner pulled off *Snow Storm*," said the Father, "because he put the right shapes and shades in the right places. Otherwise, nothing fits organically, the painting never works, and the ship goes down." I had the sinking feeling of flailing in a hole while only knowing how to dig.

"I know the feeling," said the Father. He left for a minute and returned with a pack of Belmont cigarettes, an ash tray, and a couple stick matches.

"I can't drink because I love it too much," he said. "But sometimes I allow myself a smoke."

"Gimme one of those," I said.

We spent a few minutes savoring the rush of nicotine and blowing smoke rings at *Snow Storm*.

"The story goes," said the Father, "before Turner painted *Snow Storm*, the sailors on the ship lashed him to the mast during a tempest, and he stayed there for four hours. He was sixty-seven years old at the time, and critics think *Señor* Turner's story is—"

"Embellished," I said. "We make up everything."

"Not everything," he said. "Maybe fifteen years ago, I'm driving back from the beach with my girlfriend, and we get in a wreck."

He lit a second cigarette off the first one. It didn't matter a truck had crossed into his lane, he went on, or that he and his girlfriend were drunk. He got busted up a little, but his girlfriend broke her back and spent weeks in the hospital. She survived, but their relationship died in his Jeep. He drove himself mad wondering why and how come. These are the days you never want back.

He had a flea market print of Mark Rothko's *#20* which, a few months before, he'd hung on the wall in his room.

He didn't particularly like it, but he didn't understand the painting, and he wouldn't take it down until he did. The Father brought up a photo of the Rothko on his phone, a vertical triptych of muddy-edged, rectangular blocks of burgundy, gray, and black, floating on a burnt ocher field. Even small like that, as it appeared on his iPhone screen, the Rothko felt like desolation distilled into arrows and shot straight through your heart.

"So I'm glaring at the Rothko," said the Father, "grinding myself about Camila, my life, the whole *calamidad*. And I knew those reds and blacks were exactly how I felt, and how you look right now."

"You're not helping here, *Padre*," I said.

He stared at Turner's poster and said, "I didn't fit my life. I had the wrong-colored shapes in all the wrong places, the proportions were grotesque and I felt ashamed over the failure of things and how it was all my fault. But I couldn't change what I could only feel. I had to *see* myself first."

He set down the poster, poured us both a coffee, walked me back to *El Salón de Bolívar* and we stood there, gazing stupidly at *Espacio Puro*, the gaudy gilt frame with the glass pane inside, and the bare wall showing behind it. I knew what Father Javy was going to say. That he wished there was some way to go back and undo the past, but there wasn't. That, for all the anguish and fucked-up stuff in the world, we had every right to leave it all behind. Rise like two angels and—but I wasn't an angel, and he said no such things. He pointed at *Espacio Puro*.

"Whatever I can't handle," he said, "including myself, I stick it in there. Into the void. Saints can live there; I only know how to visit. Fifty times a day, if I have to."

"I thought you people prayed," I said.

"Same difference," he said. "The frame is just a prop." I went to complain, to tell him to speak plain English for once, but he cut me off at the pass. "Look at the shit that happens to us, and the stupid stuff we do," he said, leaning into it. "Make sense to you?" He stepped toward *Espacio Puro* and glared into it. "We're stuck in the *mierda, hombre.* Crazy thing is, even Rothko didn't want to escape it. He clung to deep purple and killed himself. Dozens went out that way. What else you gonna do when you're trapped in a painting. Or a marriage." He lipped another Belmont, but didn't light it. "The letting-go is harsh," he said.

"You ever miss..." I started to say.

"Women?" said Father Javy, finishing my thought. "Of course, I do. And a lot of other things besides. But nobody gets it all."

We silently looked back at *Espacio Puro*, two men who had ever but slenderly known themselves.

"Give me another one of those smokes," I said.

Club staffers had laced together a quilt of tarpaulins that lined the floor of The Rotunda, a large open space reserved for dances and holiday fiestas. White paper sheets big as king-sized beds (courtesy of Ulises Montenegro), normally used for billboards, were stacked on the tarps in a dozen separate piles. Alongside were buckets, trays, and squeeze bottles of paint in twenty colors, along with rollers, brushes, ladles, putty knives—most everything found in an abstract artist's quiver. More than three hundred people had turned out to watch the amateur artists make a mess, all hands fortified by the open bar. The Mayor of Carabobo, with her sparkly red dress and librarian's glasses, formally announced Art Day. Then Father Javy briefly addressed the crowd.

"So what's up with this abstract stuff?" he said. "I look at this work like seismographs, each piece recording the deepest feelings of the people who paint them. Watch how the process takes on a life of its own. When you feel it happening, let the artists know. Thinking is easy. Baring your soul is not. Have fun, *mis amigos*."

Father Javy shared a few more thoughts with the contestants, who must have arrived believing a horn would sound or *galerón* ballads would play and they could start slinging paint. Now, they were obliged to cut themselves open and bleed onto the big white leaves, for all the world to see.

Each contestant got a number corresponding to a given stack of big paper leaves on the floor of The Rotunda. Minutes passed as they stared at the empty pages. Pollock and Kline might be phonies, but none of the amateur artists could just then call them cowards. Finally, Ximena O., a soap opera star, with a brush in each hand, began stabbing the paper with salvos of orange and aquamarine.

She switched to rollers, a trowel, back to brushes. She kicked off her pumps and ground her feet into puddles of purple and flame orange, stomping, beating her fists on the fierce montage. The crowd hung right there with her, hooting and cheering. Art Day had lift off.

Others went into action mode, and their painting became performance art, tending toward chaotic swirls and color slashes. Others meticulously orchestrated a rainbow of trickles and cascades. The Archbishop of Barquisimeto, in glossy lavender vestments, was apparently performing an auto-exorcism. Sky and sea, cars and crocodiles, no longer had color. The Archbishop did, and he flung small dollops of green and purple onto the big white paper.

The manager of *Navegantes del Magallanes*, the local professional baseball team, off-loaded a decade's worth of first-round losses with crimson splatter and ferocious sweeps with a house painter's brush. This pine tar Prometheus had ripped off his uniform and was shouting back from the canvas. Cameramen moved in close on faces, zoomed into exploding collages, nobody owing one damn thing to art history, each artist a movement of one.

I started talking with a priest friend of Father Javy's, a neurologist and fellow Jesuit who lived in a small rectory close by my house. He wasn't your mother's priest, or doctor. Father Áxel—like many newly-minted *médicos* from my daughter's graduating class—had a colorful sleeve tattoo on his left arm, and spent his little free time surfing in *Puerto Caballo*. He spoke English like a Bronx hipster because he did his residency—on the church's dime—at NYU's Grossman School of Medicine.

We watched the crowd huddled 'round, exhorting the artists, who were splattering, dripping, dabbing ocher, violet, shock pink. The crowd clapped wildly at a courageous show of colors; the tone grew solemn when the purple and black were laid on thick.

"Freakin' Javier," said Father Áxel. "He starts with a stupid picture frame to get the people talking. Two months later, he's got half the state curious about Krasner and Miró." Abstract graffiti had started appearing on barrio walls, he said.

I felt my spine stiffen. 10 feet past the big stone wall encircling El Club, people were eating dog food while we drank single malt scotch and watched bankers and soap opera stars pretend to be artists. I'd never helped the poor in any meaningful way, but I kept ranting on Father Áxel, who'd taken vows of poverty and worked in a clinic with sheet metal walls. But fuck it all, I'd soon have to leave this place with my dignity shot and my heart in a gunny sack. And I couldn't do jack about it. I didn't need Rothko or de Kooning. And neither did our neighbors eating dog food. Such bullshit. *Bullshit*!

"When I start hating on myself," said Father Áxel, watching me do as much, "I need something that comes from the outside. Outside time and space—and me. Some basic compound that glues all this together."

I grumbled and said, "Do all you Jesuits talk like that?" I talked like that myself sometimes, or tried to.

"Love," he said. I cringed, and wanted to stab somebody, and he said, "Something has to matter."

"Well, yeah," I said. "And what happens when it falls out?"

"It all falls out," he said. He wasn't being glib. He didn't like it either, and didn't try to explain. Neither did Mark Rothko, who wrote no suicide note before slicing the artery in his right arm with a razor blade. Maybe his *#20 was* a suicide note. I'd watched world champions self-destruct like that. They'd dead-end—starving, spent, and scared—at a crumbling headwall of rock, or an impossible river crossing, and fold. You couldn't tell them that everything falls out, including dead-ends and despair, if you can keep your eyes wide open and hold your center till it does.

My eyes were shut. I had no center. I felt like a scarecrow in the desert.

The artists were played out by early afternoon. Ximena's canvas was a vehement street fight portraying her childhood in Ecuador, she said, staring at nothing, when people preyed on her, and she did bad things. "It inspires you to love," said Father Javy, who I hated for being my friend. The other pieces were equally personal, but marginally worked as art. The diamond in the rough belonged to General Jose Malpica-Lopez, from the air force base in Maracay. No one paid him much attention, till they saw what he'd done: a graduated pane of color, each tone seamlessly applied by roller and brush, beginning with a deep green foreground, melding into light blue, darkening to indigo as it rose, merging with charcoal and finally, coal black. And at the top, glimmering dots which might have been stars.

After the booze took hold and the crowd scattered off toward the lake, Father Javy and I listened in as Estela Fontana interviewed the General for *El Carabobeño.*

He'd been a pilot all of his adult life, he said, but when his eyes started to go a decade before, they'd clipped his wings and made him a general. But the sky was where he belonged, so that's what he'd rolled onto the canvas, starting with his takeoff from green savanna, up through open blue sky and higher, into the darkness of space.

"I look at this now and a weight sinks into my heart," said the General, staring at his autobiography, "and I do not feel I shall soon stop carrying it. But there're valuable things on the ground right now, and I have to take my place here."

The sky was home. It might always feel like home, despite the heavy weather, but he no longer fit there like before. He took a final glance at the green fading to blue, to black, and he shuddered from that clammy sense of loss when something ends. Then he walked out of his painting and marched away. He never looked back.

Workers started collecting the buckets, trays, and bottles of paint, the rollers, ladles, and putty knives, as others got busy rolling up the big, colorful paper leaves and jamming them into a dumpster. I went to stop them and Father Javy grabbed me as I blurted out that things couldn't end like that. You can't fucking pour yourself into something and just wad it up and chuck it. Something has to accrue. Something had to last. The Father held fast till I blubbered out my outrage and confusion—that my life had no vanishing point, so we lived it up at El Club, trying to get even. Soon it'd be the poor people's turn. Everything falls out.

We gathered our few things, started walking for my car, and paused at a table set aside for snacks—little baskets of chips and *dulces*, and *arepas con jamón*, mostly gone except for the better part of the ugliest wedding cake ever made. The little plastic bride-and-groom cake topper had sunk to the couple's knees in the toilet-brown frosting. Just below were the names "Andrés and Salomé," in suety white letters, as if squeezed out of a tube of sun block. This had to be remnants from lover's nuptials, before they, and their marriage, sunk all the way down.

"Here," said Father Javy, grabbing a knife. "Let me cut you a proper wedge of that *chingadera*."

The Father's knife rasped over the frosting, which had set up hard as Carrara marble. He kept sawing away and we started laughing and couldn't stop till we both were doubled over. Even this mock-up of forever-after had gone to shit, yet someone felt beholden to share the remains because even the doomed trumps nothing at all. In some fucked-up, turned-around way, I'd spent my whole life looking for that cake.

"Gimme one of those smokes," I told the Father. We lit two Belmonts and watched the maintenance crew power wash the last drips of paint off the floor of The Rotunda, squeegee it down the drain, and roll their carts away.

On the drive home, Father Javy confirmed what I already suspected: there'd be no second act for Art Day. The iniquitous forces that made El Club possible, and which he'd shared in his entire life, would soon tear the nation apart. There were far too many groveling in a country with the largest oil reserves on Earth. Polls showed former paratrooper Hugo Rafael Chávez Frías had a decisive lead in the pending presidential election.

A few months later, Chávez won the presidency and his *Movimiento Bolivariano Revolucionario 2000* installed a socialist government as people with money scrambled to secure their holdings and fund moves to Madrid or Miami. Father Javy's family left early on for Basque Country, Spain. The Father stayed behind. He said he had some karma to clean up. After his first year in office, Chávez began nationalizing private assets: steel mills, shopping malls, giant rural estates—and El Club.

Father Javy told me all about it over a Skype call. I'd returned to Los Angeles after slowly escaping the self-immolation of my marriage, thanks to a couple Jesuits from Valencia and a general from Maracay, who I watched turn his back on his home turf and walk straight into the void. I'd envisioned a garden party by Manet, but my marriage had looked like *Sea Storm*. I gang-planked out of there but the wind still howled, so I followed the Father's lead and quit drinking. Steady as she goes. My oldest daughter was working the summer at a Catholic clinic in a southern state (thanks to a hookup from Father Áxel), while my youngest daughter attended Central University, in Caracas. The old home front held nothing but chaos and pain. Sometimes I missed being lashed to the mast.

A few days before, said the Father, soldiers descended on El Club and took it over, something club managers had expected for months. Anything of value not bolted down had been hauled off, leaving the structures and the lake. Hours after the takeover, the military handed off the gutted club to three junior officers, who toured the grounds and discovered the museum.

Most of the faux Pollocks and Mondrians were still there, radiant in the track lights. They certainly looked like the real thing. The young officers must have thought they had lucked upon a Latin Louvre. The same *ricos* who had fleeced the restaurant of chairs and silverware, couldn't have forgotten a billion dollars-worth of art. But maybe. This was Venezuela and crazy ruled. Either way, they had to get the lowdown on the paintings. Discreet inquiries about the museum all pointed to Father Javier. The officers cornered the Father at the University, rather than summon him to the club and draw attention to their plans.

"Here they were," the Father chuckled, "hoping they'd found El Dorado and would soon be tooling around Caracas in German sedans. Sorry, Carlos..."

The art is all fake, he told them. Nothing but composite panel prints, none worth more than a couple hundred dollars.

But what about the stuff from Venezuelan artists? one officer asked. He had a handout from the museum that established those paintings as originals, and national treasures besides. So how come they couldn't find them, the local masterpieces they might covertly cash out for the magnificent Swiss watches and Italian *pantalones*?

"I knew they hadn't thoroughly inspected the museum," said the Father. "Not all of it, anyway."

But the situation remained dicey. The homegrown art was technically on loan from various museums, all since nationalized. So the Father had to bogart the paintings from Chavista "cultural ministers," who'd pawn them off as they had every other canvas they'd gotten their hands on. Only in the last few weeks had the Father found safe havens for most of the original art, secreted in El Club's museum since Chavez took power several years before. The young officers were digging into something the Father needed to keep buried.

"I had to throw them a bone," he said, and admitted to them, yes, there remained a seminal, original work in El Club's museum. The officers drove the Father there in five minutes, and he led the three young men through the gallery rooms, back to a small space attached to the main structure, and stuck the key into the lock. The piece in question came from figurative sculpturess, Palmira de la Vega, he said. The door was giving him fits. Perhaps someone had changed the locks. Finally the key turned. Father Javier threw the door open on *Espacio Puro,* hanging alone on the wall.

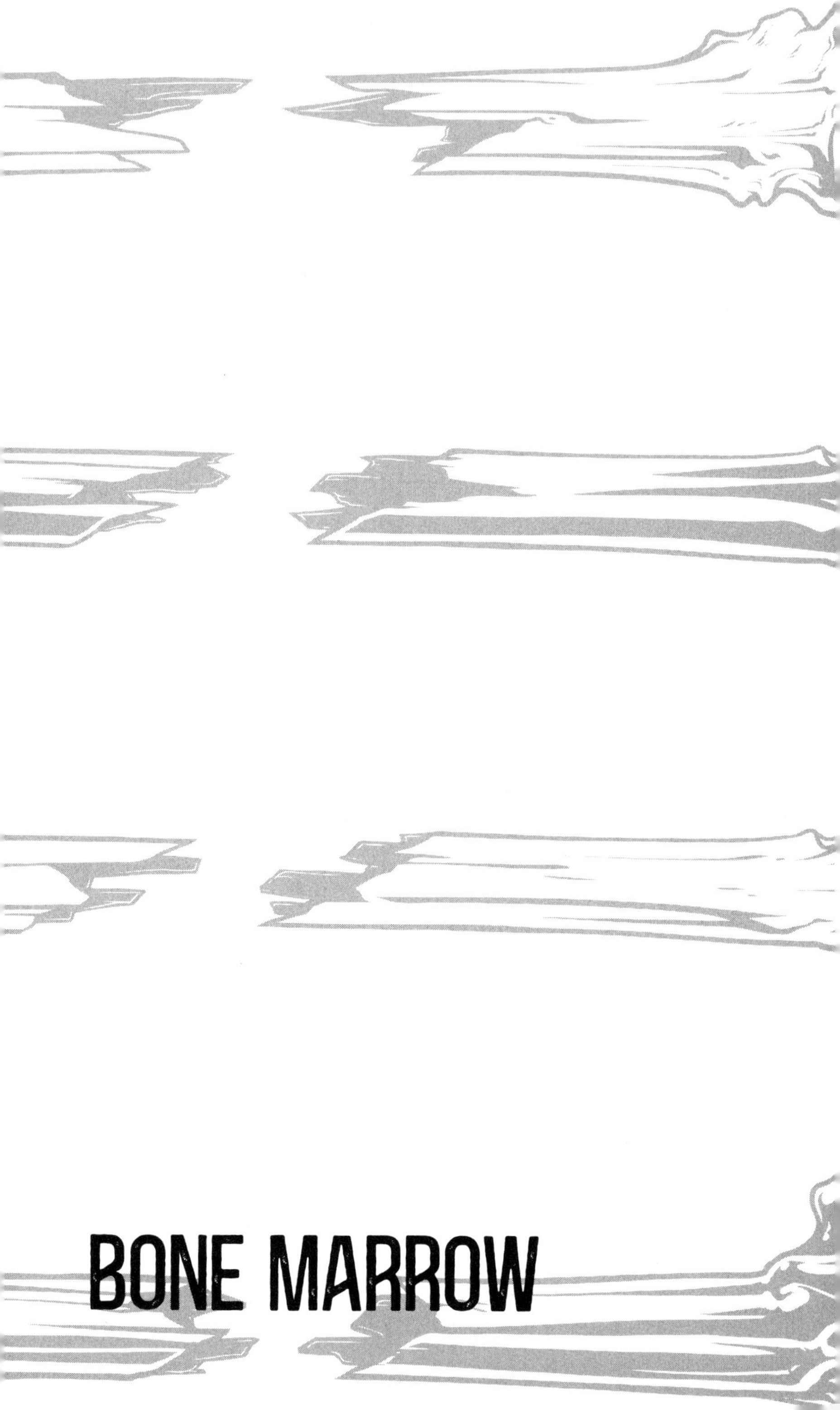

BONE MARROW

THE CONTAGION HAD FORCED us to speak with our eyes, and Flynn's riveted mine. He had a big black mask cinched so tight across his nose and mouth it might have been painted on. At ten a.m. he was the only customer sitting at one of the outdoor tables in front of Barrique, a local bistro. This was the third go-around to reopen local restaurants, since the first lockdown in April.

"You got my text," said Flynn, peering around the waiter, who set a bottle of Pellegrino, glasses, and silverware onto the white tablecloth. The plastic face shield made the waiter look like a welder in his church clothes.

"You'd be Flynn," I said.

"Donald," he said, pointing toward the empty chair at his table. I stayed standing.

From his leather brogues to his thin gold watch, Donald Flynn screamed power. I came in jeans and a sweatshirt. Flynn's fingers kept tapping the table, probably over having to meet with me after insisting on meeting with Paz. That could only happen, if it happened at all, after he correctly answered one question.

"Paz was born at Cedars-Sinai, in Santa Monica," said Flynn, going straight to it, "and she went to the Sandoval family. My wife wasn't certain about the date of adoption but, from what I gathered, it was three or four days after Paz was born."

Only the birth mother would know that. But not so fast.

"Question," I said. "Is your wife white? And nothing but?

"Of course," said Flynn. The question crooked him a little in his chair. "Might I ask— "

"Well, Paz is not, so you can't be her father. Who is?"

Flynn went blank. As though I'd asked him in Tagalog.

In some perverse way I'd come to relish these impossibly awkward moments, like two travelers who lost our wallets and got stuck in a room together. You're nobody. No name or reputation. No money to part the seas or hide behind. All you got is what you got, and I was shocked to discover how little I had sometimes.

"I've...only heard about the father," said Flynn, fumbling out the words. "Duane something. No idea what he looks like. Or Paz." Flynn grabbed the bottle of Pellegrino but was afraid to lift his mask and take a sip. "They tell me Paz was an athlete of some kind."

"The kind you used to see on magazine covers," I said. "People like her get stalked some time. Especially now."

Flynn glared, but he had nothing.

"How about we start over," I said. "Maybe start with your wife's full name. Paz would like to know that."

"My wife's a very private person," he said.

I pushed back from the table. There was shame all over this. And fear. Things Paz had dealt with her whole life.

“I don’t know how this is supposed to work,” I said, “but I won’t play the chump to your secrets. And Paz never will.”

“Confidential,” said Flynn, as a matter of fact. “No identifying information. That’s how the law reads for closed adoptions in California.”

“Same law you ignored when you dive-bombed in from nowhere, trying to get hold of Paz,” I said. “You turned her inside out—if that means anything to you.”

“I never talked to the woman,” he said, the words bursting out of him. “The only number I could find was for her agent. And how do *you* fit into—”

“Why’d you call, Flynn? What do you want?”

I should have asked him that straight off. Either way, he wouldn’t get another shot.

Flynn quietly said, “Dorothy Fournier. That’s Paz’s mother. Dorothy Ann Fournier. She’s got leukemia. They caught it early so she has a chance.”

“Jesus...” I said, as it dawned on me. “Your wife needs stem cells. From a genetic match.”

“That’s what they’re saying.”

“That’s a big ask,” I said. “This Dorothy...tell me she has other kids.”

“One son. But they’re estranged.” We kept staring at each other.

"Paz said she's never heard from the woman," I said. "Not a word. That's pretty estranged right there."

"Why don't we keep it that way," said Flynn. "I'll cover the medical. And any—"

"Aren't you the sweetheart," I cut in. "The wife hides out in Holmby Hills while you broker this like one of those organ harvesting—"

"I'm not that guy," Flynn growled, gripping the table.

"You just tried buying her off," I said. "She doesn't need your damn money, Flynn. She just wanted to know her name."

Flynn looked pale. He hiked up his mask and took a couple swallows of Pellegrino. I watched the little muscles flexing in his jaw. "I shouldn't have mentioned the money."

This turnaround came from nowhere. Without each other to push off, we only had the problem.

"I've never seen Paz like this," I said, "and I've known her since we were freshmen in college, twenty-something years ago."

Flynn's next words were so hushed I had to lean in to hear.

"Stem cells come from bone marrow," he said. "You have to drill deep to get it. No one should go through that for someone who won't even meet them."

The waiter came over, brimmed our glasses, and said,

"I'll be back in a minute to take your order."

I took a couple sips of fizzy water as Flynn removed a twenty-dollar bill from his wallet and slid it under the salt shaker.

"No you don't, Flynn," I said.

"Donald."

"You can't bum-rush me like this, then bolt."

"Bolt to where?" he said, on second thought. The only exit he had was without his wife, and he apparently wasn't that guy, either. Flynn was scared. I could feel it, all over, like the hives. I glanced at the few people, faces covered with buffs and masks, walking along the sidewalk behind us. For months, we'd hung fire as the Coronavirus raged across LA County. Now hundreds were dying a day. Yet mentioning fear was social treason. Always has been in the Home of the Brave. All those wet-plate photographs of George Washington, Thomas Jefferson and Honest Abe Lincoln. They made fortunes off whiskey, slept with their slaves, and battled clinical depression, but you'll never find a picture of them looking scared. Damn lies.

"How about we go down to the beach," I said. "Get some air." I got up and stepped away from the table, hoping Flynn would follow. He was right on my heels. We jaywalked across Ocean Avenue, followed a service road to the concrete bike path snaking over the sand, and followed it west, away from the sun.

"That restaurant was outdoors and all," said Flynn, "but I'm sixty-three. I catch that virus—"

"Should be good out here," I said, peeling the buff off my face. "Got a little breeze, even."

The wrinkled blue Pacific stretched off toward Catalina Island, heaped on the horizon 26 miles out to sea. The beach ran vacantly toward the water. Just a few knots of homeless people fiddling with makeshift shelters of plywood and old blankets they'd erected on the sand. Once we'd walked past the last small encampment, Flynn lowered his mask. He looked younger with it off.

"What do you do for work, Donald?"

"Attorney."

"Makes sense."

"Copyright law," he said. "I despise it."

"You gonna help me sort this out or keep whining?"

Flynn laughed, but it sounded horrible.

"You try and make something your business when it's not—" said Flynn. "Hell, we're like two bald guys bargaining for a comb."

"Dorothy," I said. "She'll have to talk to Paz." Flynn looked amused by the idea. "I'm getting the feeling she's a little difficult."

"Sometimes," he said. "Hard to know. I'm a little tricky

myself."

"Paz can get like that."

"You two an article?"

"We're not anything, really," I said. "She used to compete in Europe half the year, and we never could make that work. Then I went and got married and moved to Venezuela—till that blew up. When I moved back here, Paz and I took up right where we'd left off, which is nowhere."

"Gotta be something there if you're doing this," he said.

"It fizzled out years ago," I said, "but we can't quit each other. Not completely, anyhow. What's Dorothy Fournier's story?"

"She's...attractive," said Flynn.

"Got a photo or anything?"

Flynn pulled out his phone and toggled up an old photo of Dorothy Fournier in a dinner gown and jeweled earrings, standing beside a piano and smiling demurely. She had the looks much of the world chases, or begrudges. Flynn had all but said she'd drifted through life on those looks.

"Paz's tall like that," I said. "Striking, too. Just don't tell her so or she'll take it funny." A sportswriter for The Times once wrote she had those long legs you wanted to shimmy up like a native boy searching for coconuts. The writer lost his job, I said, and Paz lost her mind.

"What gives with these young people?" said Flynn. "It's just a silly a compliment."

"Maybe," I said. "But it's got too much slobber on it. So what about this son? The estranged one."

"Won't even take my calls."

"What happened?" I said. "If you don't mind me asking."

"Dorothy's my third wife," said Flynn. "Second time 'round for her, so we've tried to live forward, not back."

"You know anything, about when Paz came along?"

"Fragments," he said. "Her first husband was...trouble. Paz got adopted straightaway. Things improved, for a time, till Jeffery shows up and the marriage falls apart. I think Jeffery was born while the divorce was going through. Maybe right afterwards."

"Who got custody?"

"The father. Jeffery's never made contact with Dorothy. Far as I know."

"Doesn't sound right."

"Of course it doesn't," said Flynn. "Everybody's got something."

Doubletalk. Flynn looked a little pained. Like his shoes were too tight, but he kept walking.

"You ever see a photo of the father? Or Jeffery?"

Flynn shook his head. I had a hunch neither one looked remotely like Paz, which would have tangled up this story like barbed wire. No telling without a photo, but it got me thinking.

"How old is this Jeffery?" I asked.

"Forty-one this August."

"You sure?"

"Dorothy has the original birth certificate," said Flynn. "So, yes. That's about the only thing—" He stopped and said, "How old's Paz?"

"She turns thirty-nine in a couple months, on June eleventh," I said. "So she came last, not the brother."

That could mean a whole lot of things Dorothy Fournier had told differently, or denied altogether, to Flynn, and which he must have at least suspected. Damn lies. I punched up Paz's Wiki entry on my phone. The overhead sun burned everything out and I had to cup my hand over the little screen so Flynn could read her date of birth. He kept squinting at the date, which never changed. I stuck the phone in my pocket and we stumbled along as the random bike rolled past.

"Dorothy and Paz have a lot to talk about," said Flynn.

"Sounds like Dorothy does, anyhow."

"She won't like it, but she will," said Flynn. "Long time ago I read a book about it."

"About adoption?"

"About women who gave up their kids. They all had different stories, a thousand reasons why," he said, "but they never forgot, and they always wondered."

Paz had gone running and wasn't at her condo when I got there. Just a note saying to let myself in. It'd been ages since I was alone in Paz's place, and my eyes scanned tables and credenzas searching for shared things, special by their ordinariness. A two-dollar strip of booth photos from the Pomona County Fair, both of us wearing huge sunglasses. A Swiss cowbell from when I flew to Zurich and watched her compete in the Diamond League Track and Field Championships. Year by year, our shared things went missing—till I did, and moved to Venezuela. All that survived, in a high corner of her bookcase, was a small, hand-carved canoe with "Aloha" painted on the side, from our trip to Maui shortly after we'd first met at an Adidas event.

Paz turned up an hour later, her legs smeared with dirt, her running shirt and trunks sweated through. She'd hit the local trails for a long one. She got a bottle of Fiji water from her fridge, drank half of it and said, "So how'd it go?" trying to act casual.

"Interesting," I said. I couldn't start with the hard part,

which only left one option. "Flynn—"

"The man who called."

"Decent guy," I said. "He had a photo on his phone, of your mother." Paz looked transfixed that I'd actually seen evidence of this mythological woman. "Old photo. Pretty washed out," I said. "But she has your mouth and eyes and maybe your chin. Or you have hers. She looked tall as well."

"But she's white..." said Paz.

I hated the reckless, insane universe where a human being has to request their most intimate, personal information from a third party who has no business knowing it before they do. Paz stood there, ripped open, expectant and mortified.

"Flynn said your mother is white," I said. "Her name is Dorothy Ann Fournier. I asked about your father but he didn't know anything, and I believe him."

I'd gotten schooled by Paz about commenting on people's appearances, and the first thing we're talking about is how her mother looks. I'd brought it up, but her fascination was no wonder, not when half the people she met asked, "What *are* you, besides attractive?" Cracks like these were offered as approvals from those who deserved the facts about who they were talking to. Their questions slayed Paz, and drove her underground.

She walked across her living room and I followed her

onto the balcony, which thrust out into space from the third story, the complex rising off a ridge above Pacific Palisades. Two minutes from her door, as she'd done today, Paz could jog onto a web of dirt fire-breaks and singletracks and be alone, as she liked it, training for an hour or all day long, crisscrossing the Santa Monica Mountains.

"I should feel lucky," she said, fighting to stay above it, gazing down at the West L.A. basin as lights flickered on in a hundred thousand homes belonging to a million souls who all thought Paz Sandoval was the lucky one. If they remembered at all. "People paid me gobs of money," she said, "to run eight hundred meters a few dozen times a year. I don't even compete anymore and I've still got sponsors, this place, a few friends..." She tailed off, glanced over, and said, "Thanks for bothering with this."

"You'd do the same for me."

"Be glad I don't have to."

She never spoke about her adoption till one Christmas vacation, twenty-something years before, when she mentioned a family tree project she had in grade school, back in Laredo, Texas. She grew up there, "looking a little like everyone and exactly like nobody," I remembered her saying. She'd been raised a Sandoval, with two brothers and gracious parents. But she'd been grafted onto the Sandoval family tree and always had a deep sense she didn't really belong there, yet had no idea where her own tree was planted. Years later, her DNA profile listed

Western European, Indigenous American, Nigerian, and Filipino.

"They're only places," she'd said, staring at her pie chart on the Ancestry DNA website. "Names on a map, not people. I've never met a true relative in my life."

"You and this Dorothy need to talk," I said.

"Is something wrong?"

"You should hear it from her."

"That's not fair," she said, fiercely.

Secrets and shame. And fear. That's why people told damn lies. I was tempted, too.

"She's got leukemia," I said. "I think she just found out so it's probably not too bad. Not yet, anyhow."

Paz stood stock-still. I thought about Dorothy Fournier, whose life depended on grasping back for a daughter once forsaken and never seen again. At a time when "distancing" was not only convenient, but decreed. Paz walked over to her room and pulled the door shut behind her. I showed myself out.

I drove us to the big, empty parking lot west of the Santa Monica Pier. Paz couldn't sit still. She'd put on slacks instead of the sweatpants she lived in, and a lilac blouse that set off nicely against her bronze skin. Even put on a little makeup—rare for her.

"It's all good," I said, not believing a word of it, and glanced over as her game face formed, the bulletproof mask she strapped on before big comps. We'd stuffed our actual masks in our pockets.

The pier, vacant, jutted out into the sea. The red-and-blue gondolas hung motionless on the giant Ferris wheel. A tattered California state flag flapped on a pole. Sidewalk shops still sold postcards of the place, all lit up and alive, which felt like snapshots from a half-remembered world.

We walked onto the bike path and headed west toward the cement bench across from Lifeguard Tower 16. Paz had only gotten word from Flynn, a few hours before, that Dorothy wanted to meet at eleven. She had no time to stress out and reconsider, only to pull herself together and have me swing by.

Flynn and Dorothy came into view, sitting together on the bench 100 yards away. With each step, Paz's face grew steelier, until a stranger walked beside me, her eyes riveting the distant forms like a finish line. Without warning, a peloton of bikes roared past—Paz let out a muffled yell as they barreled by, inches away. "Fuckers!" I yelled, noticing the big blue words, BIKES ONLY, painted on the narrow cement pathway below my feet.

I lagged back as we approached the bench, Paz stopping a ways out on the path, standing straight and implacable, a bronze Diana. Dorothy Fournier, probably in her early 60s, appeared just as tall as Paz, even seated, her straight russet hair pulled back in a bun. Her face looked slightly pale, gazing from the bench with a vanishing smile.

"You're—very pretty," she said.

"What if I wasn't?" said Paz.

Maybe it was how Paz said it, from her position glaring down on the bench, but Dorothy Fournier lowered her eyes and said, "I never wanted you to see me like this."

"Is it always about you?" said Paz. Her voice was starting to crack.

Dorothy glanced up, and said, "Why, yes. It always has been. I think that may be the problem." She paused, unsure about her words, their strange directness, like a traveler trying phrases they only half understood.

Flynn got up, smiled, and offered his hand to Paz. "Donald Flynn. I'm very pleased to meet you." He didn't qualify it with "Olympian" or "exotic," which worked in his favor.

Paz looked at his hand, and shook it. Flynn wrapped his other hand over hers and said, "Thanks for coming. This takes courage." Flynn glanced at his wife and said, "Dorothy here, she's stubborn, but she'll listen to you. I promise."

The noose wrapped around us loosened a bit. An offshore breeze did the rest.

Flynn glanced at me and said, "Let's walk." We started out on the bike path, away from the bench and Tower 16. I was afraid to look back. When I finally did, the two women were sitting on the bench, a healthy space between them, but together.

"You know who you remind me of, Flynn?"

"Donald. And I'm sure I don't know."

"Paz. Can't tell you how, but you do."

Flynn said, "Hmmm," and thrust his chin toward the sea. "Always wanted to take the glass-bottom boat over to Catalina. One of our junior partners went there to bow-hunt wild boar, and shot his guide in the ass." He laughed and said, "True story."

"Nice try," I said. "Back at that restaurant, I told you Paz was a wreck and you looked like I shot *you* in the ass. You tried to lawyer up again, but you couldn't."

"I've done worse," said Flynn.

"Tell me...Donald. Who reads a book about women who give their kids away, and remembers what they said?"

He paused and gazed back at Paz and Dorothy, who'd moved off the bench and were walking slowly across the sand toward the water.

"Somebody who's adopted," Flynn finally said. "My folks knew, of course, but nobody else. It's different now. 'Bastard' is a meaningless word. But you're still a stranger to yourself."

We walked on. The peloton returned, but we saw them coming, so we stepped off the path as they stormed past like a locomotive. We kept walking.

"You ever try finding out anything?"

Flynn looked bemused, and said, "Been twenty years now, when I come up with type two diabetes. Not bad, but my doctor says he'd be pleased to know my family medical history. Of course, I didn't have any. But I knew an attorney who knew an attorney who knew a judge, who got my adoption records unsealed. I was born in San Clemente."

"Find anyone?"

"The old man," he said. "Working at the Anheuser-Busch brewery out in Van Nuys. Probably been drunk for thirty years. A Russian immigrant. I'm a Rusky." He chuckled, but it sounded all wrong. "I talked to him for a while and heard a dozen different stories about—everything. He gave me a case of Budweiser, and I left. But it was totally worth it. And this time around, with Paz, it made me remember."

He didn't say what he remembered so I asked him.

"That I'm not an attorney," he said. "I got a license. I know the job. But it's never been a match fit. Not even."

"You don't walk away from that."

"Watch me. I got some savings. Bunch of Apple stock." Flynn smiled and said, "You can color me gone."

"To where?" I asked.

"Cooking school. In Paris."

I laughed, and Flynn laughed along with me.

"You'll never go," I said.

"Probably not," he said. We laughed again.

"You think they'll work this out?"

"I trust they'll help each other," he said. "But if Paz is anything like me, she's hoping someone can tell her who she really is."

And the cow jumped over the moon. Or hoped to. "So, what now, Donald?"

"I recommend *coq au vin*," said Flynn, "with farro and couscous. And some *Chateau de Meursault*, if you can find it."

We pushed on down the bike path, which ended a short way ahead. I glanced back over my shoulder and could just make out two shimmering forms walking along the edge of the sea, where the water meets the sand.

N
NW
NE
W
E
SW
ES
S

CRAZY PEOPLE DON'T GET ICE

SHE STARED AT ME with the resolve of a bullet. I stared right back and her eyes popped and quickly shot off, as if someone behind her just screamed. Nobody had. A second later, her eyes once more locked onto me, like I was her twin brother she hadn't seen in years, walking toward Peet's Coffee in Marina del Rey, California. She winced, glanced away, then stared once more, jangled to the core—that I'd forgotten her, or didn't care either way.

I started to say, *Sorry, I'm not who you think I am*, but didn't because she looked like a junkie coming off smack. More likely she was crazy. The way her attention fractured and shot off, boomeranged back and crashed into her mind, while she fitfully wrung her hands and shifted foot to foot, aquiver in her thrift store sneakers, sweat pants, and faded Pokémon t-shirt. She must have escaped from a nut-house. Nobody so clattered ever got a day pass, or were free to just roam. She had to belong somewhere.

I needed caffeine, so I moved toward the entrance as several others hurried out, carrying cardboard trays full of drinks and pastries, blocking my view of the crazy girl. But I carried her face in my mind: her sloe blue eyes, her buzz-cut hair you might find on a convict. I put her at 25. Who named her? Where did she go on Thanksgiving? Maybe someone so fraught doesn't even belong to themselves. No matter. If she hadn't put me on the spot with her barefaced stare I'd have never looked her way. She was tough to watch, but none of my business. *Que serà, serà.*

There she was again, hovering a ways back from the door, her eyes still locked on me, like I owed her my attention. I glared back, feeling put upon. The girl needed some sand—the self-contained grit so prized by the old cowboys, all alone on the range and fine with it, none thirsty for the notice of others. Whatever. You can't coddle a psycho. I stepped toward her.

I hardly slept last night and I'm busy as hell so quit staring and making me squirm. Here. Take this dollar. Don't care how you spend it so long as it buys my escape and you become nothing again. Life isn't fair. You got what you want so beat it.

That's what I thought but didn't say, because I didn't sense she wanted money, which is all I was willing to give. I shot her a flinty look; her head turned away and I pushed past the pesky panhandler guarding the front entrance, walked to the counter, and ordered a coffee. Strong and black. Like the cowboys used to drink.

I peered into the display case at the croissants, ham-and-egg sandwiches, and craft juices, artfully positioned on a bed of mottled ice. And the crowd, in a dozen shades and flavors, so casually arrayed around the clean, well-lit room. Each of us so smartly à la mode, faces glued to touchscreens wired into a felicitous net of give-and-take. Days fashioned from little jotted-out messages and selfies insisting we lived hugely and our curated likeness and arty pap meant something to all mankind. I was bitter as French roast, but nobody could see it so they didn't know.

A barista called my name. I snagged my coffee and immediately gulped because I'm impulsive—and burned the shit out of my tongue. I glanced around in case anyone saw, annoyed by the smugness of this crowd, taken by the trance of being "woke." But cut the Wi-Fi or let the almond milk go cold and watch us show our teeth. There were well-intentioned souls in every direction, but few of us had much sand. I wasn't half bad at faking it, but I was balanced on a switchblade.

I took a discreet sip of joe, clueless that COVID-19 lurked behind the espresso machine and soon we'd get dump-trucked into our homes, no exit. How quickly we'd close the gap on the crazy girl.

I walked back outside and straight into the girl, who reeled back to a safe distance and vibrated in place. After a few false starts she said, "Can you help me? I need something to drink."

Up close she looked surprisingly clean, and smelled like French lavender soap. She had no right to stare through my chain mail like that, but how petty that all felt now.

"What would you like?"

"Maybe...a coffee."

"Take this one," and I handed her the cup. "I added a little milk, to take the curse off it."

I said all this before remembering I was talking normally with a crazy person, whose body seemed out of sync with her mind. I'd watched her wires crossing at a distance, and it chilled me to see this up close. How she'd level her eyes on me, fighting to hold her ground when some internal vortex kept spinning her gaze away, wrenching her clear of her right mind and through the circus mirror. She'd sync up again and glance back at me, panicked by the drop-out and sudden reconnect. The sharpest pain was in the repetition and the torment it caused her. Like one of Dante's Lost Souls, cannibalized by beasts and then reconstructed to be eaten again. How could she glitch and shudder and still talk with no hitch in her words or phrasing? And why did she keep staring like she knew me? Who abandoned this woman to pester busy people like myself? But I wasn't busy, only powerless. I'd dropped off a watch to have the battery replaced, so time meant little till I returned to Swiss Wrist and got busy again.

I studied the rune of her face, but couldn't read it. Someone so jejune and loopy was only a threat to herself, so I couldn't cotton to fearing her. I loathed fear, or maybe I worshiped it. Either way, it ruled me. I motioned towards several empty tables on the sidewalk.

"How 'bout we sit for a second," I said. "I got some time. A little, anyhow."

She didn't move, holding the coffee close to her chest. I sat and held her gaze as calmly as I could. I'd bully myself, and often did, but I couldn't bully this girl. It'd never work on someone so gun-shy. I tried to talk over the gray road she'd followed to get there, the potholes and the wrecks that showed in her clothes, her eyes, and her reeling. I told her my name and watched her sidle toward a chair in fits and starts. Finally she sat, her eyes briefly locking on me before jerking away, back on me and off again. Her bony frame jumped each time, like someone ripping Band-Aids off their face.

"So, what's your name? From around here?"

She didn't say a word. I talked about myself, rounding off the edges and fashioning a person who never existed in the way I described him. Not a peep. The disturbing way she clenched her fists and slow-writhed in her chair slowly eased the moment I stopped talking and trying to *do* something. Maybe she didn't appreciate my efforts to help. But if silence was her ballast, what did she need me for?

A truck backfired on the road and we both jumped.

"That scared me," she said.

"Scared me too," I said.

She looked at me again, a private gaze she held for a beat before her eyes tore away once more. Little tics still shot through her, but that flash of clear sky in her eyes was enough to light the sonder. Somehow, the person sitting across the table experienced her life with the same boggling range that I did. That we all did. Streaming along the sidewalk, rolling along the road, thrummed a lurid samba rich and bereft. This girl was so thrown-open the whole thing physically moved her which, through contagious example, lowered my drawbridge and it all came rushing at me. The *Salvadoreño* with the leaf blower; the kid with a plastic sword in one hand and a yellow balloon in the other, running like a ram along the sidewalk. And the older lady who stole a parking space, pissing off the bottle-blonde behind her who jumped from her Jeep and slammed the door, unaware of having the luxury to choose her problems.

"I can't drink this," said the crazy girl, pushing the

coffee across the table. "It's too hot."

"'Cause they brew the shit at two thousand degrees," I said. "Just a sec."

I went inside the coffee shop and got a small cup of ice. What might the barista say had the crazy girl requested the same? Crazy people rarely have money so they don't count and better get lost. I imagined a sign on the wall: *SANE PEOPLE ONLY*. Crazy people don't get ice.

We dropped a few frosty cubes into the coffee and took turns drinking it. I'd lost the need to talk, and she never spoke again. Her dark energies stopped arcing so hard. Only the random shudder. When her hand took the cup from mine, I saw little remnants of glittery polish on several nails. At some other time and place, prettification mattered. Was she ever on someone's guest list? Were there Amber Alerts for crazy people? And what did crazy actually mean? Then none of that mattered.

Sitting there with the anonymous girl felt like being inside a tear, light sparks darting from the surface. I didn't want to leave. As we passed the *venti* coffee cup back and forth, I could feel and hear my clunky character, how it used words like *crazy* to label another human being, and *girl* instead of young woman. This byzantine, conflicted contraption of me. No neutral. No reverse. Blown head gasket, so prone to overheating. And no brakes, so damn near impossible to stop. Till I found myself floating. The stillness startled me.

The young woman, casually sipping the coffee, no longer twitched or stared at me, as I no longer stared at myself. We sat there, linked by a bridge of sighs. How long had she imagined this song without words, only heard when shared? How had she known to share it with me? Such a lark, this random stray in her thrift store clothes. But for a moment, fraying at the edges, she might have been the ideal human being.

We finished the coffee and I had to get my watch. She walked with me to Swiss Wrist, a few blocks away. Step by step, the distance stretched between us and the demons took her back. I left her on the sidewalk, hands clenching, eyes wrenching to and fro, and went in to get my watch. When I came back out, she was gone.

ICARUS SYNDROME

"HOW FAR'D SHE FALL?"

"Far enough to blow the helmet off her head," said Tom. "Rescue team short-roped her off the wall, and they airlifted her out. Don't see how you survive that fall, but she did—somehow."

We'd just arrived in Yosemite Valley for a video shoot, finding Tom Evans in a corner of the cafeteria, editing photos from the rescue, which he took from El Capitan Meadow using his "big gun" telephoto lens. Whoever is climbing El Capitan, Tom shoots them for his *elcapreport.com* ("Unique in all the World!"), highly prized by Valley cognoscenti, and which Tom updates every evening in his van. Tom paused on a shot of the chopper in midair, the tan bulk of El Cap rising in the background. At the end of a rope far below the chopper, rescue ranger Brandon Lathum and climber Quinn Brett—who was strapped into the litter—dangled in space like spiders on a string.

"Speed climbing the Nose?" I asked.

"What else?" said Tom. He looked ill.

Word trickled in over the following days. Quinn broke four ribs, punctured a lung, and bruised her liver in the fall. She also suffered a burst fracture of her twelfth thoracic vertebra, "typically a severe spinal injury," according to her doctors. If they knew how severe, no one was saying. Friends started a *YouCaring* campaign, donations streamed in from a dozen countries, but still no word on Quinn's prognosis. Two months and three operations later, while rehabbing at Doctors Medical Center in Modesto, California, Quinn started blogging:

Will I ever walk hand in hand with Max again? WALK hand in hand. BE with Max? Live a life without diapers and worrying about shitting in the middle of the night because I have no control?

WHAT THE FUCK!

This from the woman who popped handstands on gusty Patagonian summits, who ran "Rim to Rim to Rim" (45 miles, 22,000 feet elevation gain/loss) in the Grand Canyon, and raged up dozens of Yosemite big walls, several in record time. She was a spark on the tinder of American adventuring until, on a speed climbing run on the Nose route of El Capitan, she fell 100 feet and body slammed off another flake below. Now, she was paralyzed from the belly button down.

Sometimes I am depressed, wonder if I should be here. I can't believe that this is where I am at. I am scared. I am sorry. I am overwhelmed.

Reading these words at home in Venice Beach, California, I pushed back from my desk as a long-forgotten scene bubbled into memory. I studied the photos in Quinn's blog—the heinous road rash, the Frankenstein gash from spinal fusion surgery—and thought to myself, "Oh, shit... That could have been me."

Memorial Day, 1975. Seven years before Quinn was born. Jim Bridwell, Billy Westbay (both lost from us now), and I cast off to attempt the first one-day ascent of the Nose, the world's most sought-after rock climb.

"Pull this off and we'll never live it down," Jim laughed as we geared up in the dark at the base of the wall. Twice that year, teams had attempted the NIAD (Nose in a Day), bonking in the upper corners, half a mile over the trees. I tied into the rope and charged, hell-bent. I was 21 years old. Shortly past dawn, I pendulumed right into the Stoveleg Crack, a laser-cut slash bisecting the sweeping granite nose where the southwest and southeast faces converge. The ground dropped away as pitches (rope lengths) that normally took an hour were dispatched in minutes, a speed achieved through placing little to no protection. Jim promised plenty of fixed nuts and pitons in the crack but there weren't any. The climbing was steep and thuggish, but secure, so it didn't matter. Going fast was all that mattered.

By seven a.m., now a third of the way up the wall, I stormed up a ladder of bolts drilled into the rock, gunning for Boot Flake, a 50-foot granite scab describing a boot if you eye it dead-on from El Cap Meadow. I'd climbed The Nose once before and remembered the crack along the Boot's right side as secure but off-balance. I chalked up and started tomahawking my hands into the wavy crack. The first 20 feet felt solid so I pressed on, not bothering to place protection in the crack and waste time, jamming for the shelf and bolt anchors atop the Boot. Nearly there, my left arm cramped and my hand curled into a claw. I hadn't hydrated enough. I shook my frozen arm, my right hand creeping from a greasy hand jam.

My eyes darted down 50 feet to my last protection. When I pitched off—not if, but when—I'd cartwheel down the wall and smash into Texas Flake, the jagged-edged atoll where Jim and Billy were moored, 100 feet below. I wasn't thinking about getting busted in half or even dying, but the shame of dreaming so big and coming up so small. That I was a pretender all along.

I glanced at my jammed hand, melting from the crack. I had one big hexcentric on my rack and, when the cramp released for a second, I fumbled the nut into the crack, clipped in the rope, and slumped onto it. Cold sweat streamed down my neck as the mango-sized nut pivoted in the crack. I shook my arm out, reset the nut, and groped up the last 10 feet to the shelf and the anchors. It was 7:20 a.m. Billy grabbed the lead, streaked across the "Gray Band" of diorite that girds El Cap and, before I could catch my breath, the vortex of our speed ascent sucked me off the anchors and across the wall, blowing away my near miss on Boot Flake. But I'd fucked up hugely and squeaked by on luck, nothing else.

Forty-three years later and I'm cowering in the Oval Room at the Fairmont Copley Plaza Hotel in Boston, Massachusetts, hearing about the fall I should have taken by the climber who took it—at the exact same place on Boot Flake.

"Tell me about the climb," asks Ashley Saupe, hosting

The Sharp End podcast. I'm at the annual American Alpine Club gala and the band's all here, male and female, heroes and has-beens, spanning generations, everyone strands in a web stretching from the Oval Room to Yosemite Valley to the Himalayas and beyond.

Quinn gazes at Audrey with liquid brown eyes and says, "Last time I'd been in Yosemite with Hayden Kennedy, he'd taken a big fall off Pancake Flake halfway up the Nose during a speed push. And he came down and had a giant hematoma on his hamstring, and he and I sat by the river, and he soaked his leg and talked about how that felt. Like, he took a sixty-footer and was freaked out and he said, 'Quinn, I don't know why we're doing this speed climbing thing.'"

He was doing what athletes always do at the thin end of the wedge: try and break new ground. A competent team at a casual pace can climb El Cap trade routes with trepidation, but little fear for their lives. Hundreds do so every season. Smoking those same routes, however, chasing a record time, means no pausing to strategize, to place adequate protection, or drop anchor and regroup, however briefly. You simply charge, hell-bent, using your experience and instincts as collateral. Gravity never sleeps, so the potential danger is towering. It's also optional, and a throbbing rope burn can make even crushers like Hayden Kennedy wonder, *Why?* The question is part of the web, though hidden at first. As the adventures run together and seasons pass, partners, friends, and acquaintances drop into the void so abruptly that it rips holes in the web. The question lives in those holes, holes that can swallow light.

The day before Quinn and Josie McKee head up on the Nose, they learn that Hayden, 27, and his girlfriend, Inge Perkins, 23, had gone backcountry skiing below Imp Peak, Montana, when a hard slab avalanche plowed down a gully and buried them alive. Hayden dug himself out but he couldn't find Inge. She was gone. The next day, lost in the dark, Hayden killed himself.

"When Josie and I pulled into El Cap Meadow, the morning of our climb," says Quinn, as the podcast rolls, "I was texting my boyfriend about Hayden, struggling with his death. Josie and I were like—we'd planned on climbing the Nose so let's just go. So, out of habit, we put on our climbing gear and, out of habit, we walked to the base because that's what we did. Climb. Fast. Next thing you know we were going."

After 1975, the NIAD remained an infrequent feat performed mostly by Valley locals. Speed climbing, as a movement, caught speed in 1990, when former pole-vaulting star "Hollywood" Hans Florine made speed climbing his life work, scaling El Cap over a hundred times, setting speed records on most every route he bagged. His definitive statement came in 2014, while partnered with Alex Honnold (who later won an Oscar for *Solo*, the highest grossing documentary in history, about his no-rope ascent of El Capitan in 2018). The pair lowered the Nose speed record to a blazing two hours and forty-six minutes. His 2015 release, *On the Nose: A Lifelong Obsession with Yosemite's Most Iconic Climb*, was a bestseller in the outdoor industry. His record with Honnold seemed beyond reach.

Women joined the hunt in the 1990s, though many felt female promise was scarcely tapped until 2011, when Libby Sauter and Chantel Astorga took down the Nose in 10:40 (the record had stood at 12:15 for a decade or so). Brett and Jes Meiris responded, clocking in at 10:26. Later that summer, Mayan Smith-Gobat and Chantel Astorga lowered the time to 7:26. In 2013, Smith-Gobat, partnered with Sauter, starched the route in 5:39, in 5:02 the following spring and, later that fall, set the current speed record at 4:43 (surely one of the greatest and least-recognized feats in female sport). Of the many who've climbed El Cap in a day, only a handful ever chased records.

The morning after Quinn's accident, I drove to El Cap meadow and found Tom hunkered behind his camera. For all who have climbed El Capitan, the meadow exerts a gravity that pulls you into a little gravel clearing by a stunted pine, close by the Merced River, where Tom takes his photographs and climbers loiter in random groups, or wander off alone and stare at the monolith. From that distance, the wall is still a long way off, but at 3,000 feet high and several miles wide along the base, it seems like you can reach out and touch it. You sit there and bask in its raw basal force, recalling life up high, and your spells of dark brood when you'd wonder why you were working harder than you ever worked in your life, beating down the fear when below there were tanned tourist girls to chase and beer to drink and sandy riverbanks to lounge on and do nothing—and everything. But it was a dull wonder you couldn't answer with ideas. The answer plunged below you on the rock: you were climbing El Capitan.

Most of the ragged ensemble I found in the meadow had been on hand for Quinn's rescue, and the atmosphere felt grim. Brad Gobright wandered over. 29 and cool as an iceberg, Brad had climbed for twenty-one years, hiking world-class climbs across the Western States, often without a rope. A native Southern Californian, like myself, Brad also grew up clawing over the grainy quartz monzonite domes out at Joshua Tree National Park, a high-desert destination area north of Palm Springs. The previous fall, he'd climbed the Nose half a dozen times with partner Jim Reynolds, and eleven more times that season, honing their game for an all-out run at the speed record. I asked Brad what he thought happened to Quinn on Boot Flake. His eyes never left El Cap. "No idea."

No disrespect to Quinn intended. The man was locked in, scanning the rock like a predator, absorbed in his own private calculus. His partner, Jim Reynolds, had said in an interview, "The closer we're getting to the record, we're pushing the boundary between dangerous and reckless just a little bit more. So we're starting to wonder: can we just take a little bit more risk and get it finished, so we don't have to come back and take all that risk again?"

Eleven days later, Brad and Jim Reynolds pulled the trigger. Gobright led from the ground to the top of Boot Flake, 1,300 feet up the wall, placing but three cams over that distance. They smoked the route in 2:19:44, breaking Honnold and Florine's record by four minutes.

In Josh Lowell's and Peter Mortimer's feature-length documentary, *The Nose Speed Record,* Honnold later said: "When Brad and Jim did the record, at the top they had an entire 60-meter rope between them but nothing clipped, no gear between them, and Brad was literally just holding onto the bolts with his fingers. And I'm like—what are you guys doing?!" The inference being that Alex and Hans levitated up the Nose on savvy and legerdemain, while Gobright and Reynolds burgled the record through recklessness. Brad, amongst the world's most accomplished big wall free climbers, played along because he knew better.

"Alex tells me, 'Dude! You guys are really sketchy,'" said Gobright. "I'm like, 'Yeah. It's sketchy. But that's why I got the record...and you don't.'"

The following fall, Gobright perished in a rappelling accident while climbing in Mexico, and Reynolds astonished the adventure world by climbing up and down 4,000-foot Mt. Fitzroy, in Patagonia, with no rope.

"What about your fall off Boot Flake?" asks Ashley.

We're half an hour into the podcast and half the crowd looks ready to run. Quinn straightens and describes reaching the crack, and how the rope gets stuck below but there's a great loop of slack out in her lead rope, so she starts jamming out the Boot with no belay, "because that's the way you climb the pitch. Josie yells up that we're at two hours, which is, like—sick. We're on a really cruiser pace."

As Quinn nears the top of the Boot, Hayden Kennedy flashes through her mind. She gropes for a camming device, slung to her harness, which she might slot in the crack in an emergency. Like now. Except she's dropped the cam. Or maybe placed it already. She isn't sure which. Only that everything is racing south. Just as it'd gone for me, and for dozens of others present who've battled impossible moments and inexplicably escaped, while Quinn did not. A dreadful few among us are sole survivors, and sit still as salt statues as Quinn recounts the moment: feet paddling, hanging for her life on Boot Flake, fumbling gear and thinking, "'I shouldn't do that,' or, 'I shouldn't have done that.' One second of a feeling like in an elevator," says Quinn. "Then—falling. Thankfully, I don't remember the rest."

Quinn briefly reviews the rescue operation (a more technical extraction is hard to imagine), and Ashley asks how her recovery is going.

"It's been a pile of shit," says Quinn, "and it's been amazing, with the people who've come to help me." Audrey mentions the *YouCaring* fund-raiser, how strangers from Kenya to Israel have given over $125,000. Quinn's game face, courageously worn so far, shatters and falls. "I did a stupid thing, and people are helping me and it's pretty amazing. So, thank you very much."

We muster smiles. Offer encouraging words. But the tension won't break till we stop our perverse well-wishing and finally sync up with Quinn, with all our dread and broken edges. And the inexorable sundown of feeling hits home to the many present whose partners and friends have fallen through the net, leaving gaping holes, which stir with the dead. For a suspended moment, as the past breaks out in our hearts, the Oval Room is a house of catharsis. Scattered applause breaks the trance, and none too soon. I'll give the crisis this palliative minute, as a tribal rite. But forget boring down to causes and conditions to discover where I truly stand—about Quinn, speed climbing, any of it—because I'm not yet ready to wrestle that beast.

I peer at the clouds, artfully brushed on the ceiling. Legend says that circa 1905, after John Singer Sargent finished the murals in the iconic Boston City Library across the street, he dropped by the Oval Room and painted an angel on the ceiling. I can't find it. Searching around, I find the next best thing: Libby Sauter, with her bucket-full of freckles and a smile off a toothpaste ad. She's one of Quinn's partners from way back, and spent nearly all that first month at her bedside. Libby splits time between cutting-edge adventuring (a skilled slackliner and ultrarunner, she currently holds speed climbing records for the Nose, Salathé Wall, and Lurking Fear routes on El Capitan—the latter bagged with Quinn), and working as a war zone cardiac nurse in places like Benghazi, Libya.

Libby Sauter never plays it safe.

As Libby and I join the crowd moving through the exit, my smile feels like a clown mask. What is this, a celebration or a wake? By what crazy fluke are we even alive to be here, especially the alpinists and big mountain folk who dominate this crowd. Seen from the perspective of my Venezuelan-born daughter, a Latina pediatrician who donates her time to Doctors Without Borders, what gives with these callow white yahoos and their hoary legacy? What would all the dead say to our back-slapping and tequila shooters in their honor, as those left bereft in their wake ask why for the rest of their lives?

"My West Point class must have a thousand man-years of combat at this point," former soldier and Patagonia climber, Gregory Crouch, emailed me that morning, "what with Panama, Desert Storm, and all that shit in Afghanistan and Iraq, and we have one person Killed In Action. Of the people with whom I've shared the rope in my thirty-five years of climbing, seventeen of them are dead. It's like the Somme."

Most mountaineers want only to bag a giant peak and survive a blockbuster, but few venturing onto big, technical mountains have not repeatedly feared for their lives—and they charge regardless. Climbing as fetish. But I'm a rock climber, where the picture is brighter. Unless you venture to stormy venues like Patagonia, in southern Argentina; talent and technology have largely brought the hazards under control, especially in pacific areas like Yosemite. To peer over the edge, a rock climber must solo or speed climb, or intentionally chase other dangers. The stated goal, as it goes for most alpinists, is to reap remarkable experiences, or perhaps, set a record, capture the public's eye, and get a sponsor. Or keep one. But every avid soloist or speed climber has, at some time, seen God.

I have a room in the hotel and Libby and Quinn will use it as a staging area before the gala dinner that evening. I let the pair into my room and lift Quinn from her chair and onto the bed. She can't weigh more than a hundred pounds, her once-strong runner's legs now as slender as reeds. Her vacant eyes betray the incomprehensible disillusionment of going, in seconds, from a flower with a cannon inside, to...this. Here's a conflict I can only square at the open bar downstairs. Better head over to Copley Square and the historic Boston Public Library, a few blocks away. I'll duck into a dusty booth and look at the pictures in *Surfer* magazines.

Libby walks me back to the elevator. We both occasionally work for the same outdoor clothing brand, but we haven't spoken in months. She's still climbing, and harder than ever, she says, but on short sport routes, gym bolted and secure. Nothing like her halcyon days when she set all those speed records on El Cap, including the one with Quinn. Watching a soulmate go from able-bodied to paralysis "makes speed climbing a whole lot less cool."

The last time Libby went climbing and got way off the ground, she visualized bodies tumbling through the air. When one of the best of them all sees this in her mind, the canonical, self-prescribed heroism we sometimes ascribed to speed climbing, all that giddy valorizing, feels bogus as Halo Jones and Spiderman.

Libby will later write in *Rock and Ice* that she had been "guilty of having spread the bullshit narrative that there is a way to speed climb safely. At my peak of speed climbing on the Nose, I would do fifteen pitches on ten cams for the first block and, while it 'felt safe'—it sure as shit wasn't. I'm not telling people not to speed climb, but that kind of climbing isn't for me anymore."

"That kind of climbing" involves the leader and the second climbing concurrently ("simul-climbing") on opposite ends of a 60- or 70-meter-long rope. Once the team goes live, it's a blood oath. If the leader falls, or the second falls and pulls off the leader, the team is saved only by whatever protection they've placed between them, rarely more than one piece, since placing gear takes time and carrying it takes energy. Any fall will likely be 100 feet or more, prompting the universal credo that "you *cannot* fall while speed climbing." Advanced techniques, like short-fixing, are faster yet sketchier still. Fact is, belaying at an anchor (at the end of a given pitch, or rope length) is where a climber recovers, however briefly. Now it's like a boxing match with no bell between rounds, because there are no rounds. It's a slugfest all the way. What's more, climbing so much technical rock requires holding a surgeon's focus for hours on end; but hold it you must, between the short span of our fingertips and a sloping edge, or the climb can undo your life.

Libby's cautionary drift echoed through the adventure world at large. In an interview for *The Nose Speed Record,* Gobright said, "chasing the Nose record is absolutely dangerous. There's no getting around that." In a piece for

Outside, writer and alpinist, Kelly Cordes, noted that, no matter how you play it, the techniques used at hyper-speed are complex and potentially lethal, a process he likened to redlining a Ferrari on a winding mountain road without a seatbelt. "Everything's fine—unless you crash," wrote Cordes. "But to embody the physical and psychological competency to race up the most iconic wall on the planet in a couple of hours must feel like flying."

The flying metaphor made sense to Tommy Caldwell, Cordes' neighbor and likely the foremost large-scale rock climber in history, whose free ascent of the Dawn Wall on El Capitan in 2016 became a worldwide media event. He admitted to Cordes, "Man, I think of the wingsuit community, how at first people were like, 'If you only fly in these conditions, only fly in this terrain, it's actually safe.' And now, everybody knows that it's just dangerous, no matter what. I wonder if speed climbing is the same."

Not the same, but equally addictive. I half-seriously coined it the "Icarus Syndrome." Look at what happened to Hans Florine, who'd climbed El Cap 178 times, breaking the Nose speed record eight times. Yet at 54 years old, he still needed more. On May 3, 2018, roughly six months after Brett's podcast in Boston, Hans started up Pancake Flake, 2,000 feet up the Nose, during a scheduled, one-day ascent. A nut blew out and he crash-landed on a ledge, breaking his left tib/fib in two places and shattering his right heel. The indomitable Alex Honnold was terribly sorry for Hans, who he'd partnered with two years before to capture the speed record from Dean Potter and Sean Leary (both perished wingsuit flying), only for Gobright and Reynolds to snatch it away the following autumn. Now Florine had an external steel fixator bolted onto his leg and Honnold wanted his record back. He enlisted Tommy Caldwell's services a week after Florine's crash, and the two began running laps on the Nose, perfecting their systems and teamwork with each ascent.

"I've never been the danger dude," said Caldwell. But after a few swift burns up the Big Stone, he understood Florine's trademark refrain, that the Nose speed record "is the most badass competition there is."

"The Nose," said Caldwell, "has to be the coolest racetrack in the world." The fact it's also dangerous as hell, even for El Cap master Tommy Caldwell, struck home a few days later during another training run, when he logged a 100-foot fall off the relatively easy Stoveleg Crack. Alex fell a half an hour later, burning his hand and losing a chunk of flesh while grabbing the rope. It could have gone far worse.

"It was at least a hundred feet," said Caldwell of his fall. "I was like: I'm still falling. *I'm still falling!*"

"Hope nobody saw that shit," said Honnold. "Kind of horrifying." But after the adrenaline washed through and they slept it off, they both put their falls behind them.

On May 28, Honnold and Caldwell clocked a "relatively casual lap" in 2:25, only six minutes off Gobright and Reynolds's record pace. Two days later, they brought it home in 2:10:15, smashing the record. Might they possibly reach the "mythical milestone" and log a sub-two-hour ascent? This meant going a full five percent faster than their quickest ascent, which increased the risks exponentially. At the velocity top speed climbers were traveling, with the margin for error so thin, and with even the best logging monster falls in the process, many felt speed climbing was a game of chance, that it was impossibly lucky—and nothing less—that a team hadn't straight-up died. Several days later, on June 2, 2018, that all changed.

Tim Klein, 42, and Jason Wells, 45, had climbed together since their early 20s, and had nearly two hundred ascents of El Cap between them, including a mind-numbing forty one-day ascents of the Salathé Wall (the other El Cap route regularly speed climbed). Their accident occurred on the lower reaches of the Salathé, on moderate climbing above a prominent feature called the Half-Dollar, where the pair had passed another party. No one is certain what happened. But whatever protection and anchors they had, failed after the leader fell, and the partners experienced a terror no human needs to know, taking a 1,000-foot ride into the dirt.

Tim Klein and Jason Wells had no truck with record times. They simply loved climbing fast, and probably had more experience doing so than any team alive. But they still simul-climbed, still carried as little gear as possible, and placed it frugally. They must have believed if they intimately knew the route, and their own limits, and kept the speed a hair's breadth below maximum, speed climbing was actually safe.

Climbing Magazine waxed that "speed climbing is the inevitable expression of our basic human yearning for transcendent experience." True, but *Climbing* had taken the dramatists prerogative to milk the glory and leave out the corpses. Quinn was paralyzed, Florine was laid up in traction, and Klein and Wells were dead, both leaving wives and young children behind. The adventure world, smarting from a moral whiplash, could not so easily unpack this. Many insiders knew the fastest teams, like a conquering army, claim everything in their path. Since only elapsed time mattered, speed climbing had very narrow meaning, and could quickly become a force so destructive that even the greatest send was a pyrrhic victory, inflicting such a devastating toll on others that success was tantamount to overall defeat. Stunning performances were happening, but heroic depictions of speed climbing had many of us looking in the mirror.

Several weeks after the Salathé Wall tragedy, while cragging out at Joshua Tree, I ran into a young high-desert climber from the party Klein and Wells passed on the Half-Dollar. They had watched the pair hurtle past, and heard one of the departed screaming the entire way as he ragdolled into the ground. A gruesome experience still haunting the high-desert climber and which, for me, knocked the shine off speed climbing forever. The effects ran deeper still, but my ostrich-like avoidance of my own feelings kept me a stranger to myself. Not entirely, but when the harpies circled, I took to running. If only to the library. Caldwell, being Caldwell, knew he had to get back on the horse, but he did so with few illusions.

"With all the carnage this past year," said Caldwell, "it makes me hesitate...a bit." But the gravity of the two-hour barrier, and the thrill of the hunt, trumped his fear—which is often the case for the few who ride the gas and rarely the brake. On June 6, 2018, four days after Wells' and Klein's accident, Alex and Tommy started up the Nose at six a.m. and topped out one hour and fifty-eight minutes later.

Kelly Cordes got hold of Honnold and Caldwell on his cellphone shortly after they reached the summit. Listening over the speakerphone, he asked Caldwell if he had designs on going even faster.

"Totally done," he said.

Tommy is only an acquaintance, but I take him at his word. Meanwhile, Honnold, floating over Yosemite's scorched earth, was looking to the future, as only Honnold can. He later wrote he believes the true human potential for speed climbing El Cap is 1:30. Or even 1:15.

Two blocks down Boylston Street, and the Boston Public Library heaves into view. First the red tile roof sloping into a green copper cornice, flecked with seashells and dolphins above a frieze of classical figures—winged horses, an eagle on a branch. Below this lie thirteen arched bay windows faced with wooden Roman grillwork, painted dark to appear as iron.

Soon I'm in Copley Square, gazing across at three high arches, trimmed with wrought-iron lanterns, which form the library entrance. Out front, two allegorical female figures, cast in dark bronze and glistening in rainwater, sit on rusticated pedestals. One hooded figure, on behalf of Art, holds a palette and a paintbrush. The other, examining an orb in her hand, represents Science.

I sit on an icy park bench, trying to shake my funk, staring across at architect Charles Follen McKim's "palace for the people," a hulking Historic Landmark faced in pink granite, as though McKim built Boston their own El Capitan. Like Mecca, like Yosemite Valley, many come to pay homage. My eyes tilt up and I read the names chiseled in granite panels below the bay windows: Zeno, Plato, over to Praxiteles, on to Kepler and Laplace, settling on Da Vinci, Spinoza, and Bach. I try and picture the board of trustees who first imagined this library in the 1860s, as a Renaissance-style monument to those who kept dreaming and getting-after until the world reimagined itself.

I'll never see my name in granite, but the getting-after has sustained me when nothing else could. And I loved the fiery questing of it all. Having a *raison d'être*. Being the first human being to do *something*. From my late teens onward, my strongest sense of meaning derived from flying close to the sun, always knowing that with speed climbing and soloing, as with art, politics, and crime, it's what you get away with that counts. But every Icarus has an expiration date, and friends and family squirming on the ground, so questions lingered.

When does a competitive spirit become a reckless fling

with death? When does ambition mutate into a selfish crusade for fame? There's more to the game than these thorny dichotomies. And no question, dreaming and getting-after are as tightly woven into some of us as the apocalyptic elements of life. But I had to post my limits for the rest of my life to unfold. Even the incomparable Tommy Caldwell, who heard the rattling chains, drew a chalk line on the rock and is "totally done" with speed climbing. Otherwise, danger becomes a granite-hard drug mainlined in a haunted house with no boundaries and no value beyond itself. There lies No Man's Land. But if I had it all to do over again, I would, in a heartbeat. It's a conflict I could never live without.

"Had I summited that day [of my accident]," said Quinn Brett from her wheelchair, "I would probably still be speed climbing. I mean, it's a pretty awesome feeling." And this feeling, this experience, has little to do with records. It's a reckoning with your own limits and your capacity to act with skin in the game, on a vertical stage known as the *ne plus ultra* of natural magnitude. For those who rightfully ask why, no answer is ever enough.

DRAINS OUT THE BAD

I WAS ON THE ROAD, in western Kentucky, teaching wilderness skills for a trendy clothing manufacturer, when I met Amos. He looked a little like Marv ("I have a condition") in *Sin City*. Amos had been in and out of jail—mostly in—till he got paroled, at age 52, after doing a "dime" for sticking up a convenience store in Pewee Valley. Then he found caving, and started working with youth offenders. Amos was a freelancer, apart from any organization. Over the years, he'd gained the trust of the authorities, and they offered his short field trips to delinquents as rewards for good behavior. It worked well for all involved. Made me curious to see what Amos was up to.

Next morning, I met Amos, his two assistants, James and Norman, along with twenty-three young offenders culled from halfway houses and detox centers. Most of the class were raw, restless, and defiant. This band would normally scatter like cats, except once we were inside the cave we could only go forward, crawling and duckwalking over a mile into a Kentucky catacomb. By spelunking standards, the cavern was small beer. No rivers or sinkholes or flowstone sculptures. Names peppered the 500 feet of cave, spray-painted across the walls and ceiling, our sneakers crunching on a sea of broken bottles. We soon dead-ended in a big, sandy floored cave room that looked and felt like a dungeon.

Amos instructed his "fellow delinquents," as he called them, to spread out and lay back in the sand, the beams of their headlamps crisscrossing in the darkness, barely reaching the ceiling 40 feet overhead.

“Ok,” said Amos, “on the count of three, y’all turn off your headlamps.” The moment the lights went out murmurs, whispers, and eventually a scream rang out. In a deep cave like this one, you can’t see your hand in front of your face. One guy flipped his headlamp back on: all the others followed. Amos said to turn off all headlamps again, challenging them. Only seconds passed before twenty lights flicked on. Those who couldn’t take it were led out to the light by James and Norman, who took them on a hike. This winnowed the class to three: a young black girl and two white guys in their mid-20s, covered with jailhouse tats.

Amos later told me only a few in any group can stand the silence and darkness, and those are the few he could help. In the years he’d been guiding addicts and offenders into caves, over fifty people had been “saved” by the silence. Not by itself, of course, but the experience was profound enough the other modes of recovery could take hold. Perhaps for kids whose history is full of stones, the past weighs so heavily on them they can never escape it; but the darkest past is crushed by the stillness of the void. Most reel. A precious few experience a flash of freedom never imagined. A little, to be sure, but castles are built on a sliver of hope.

“Somehow, it drains out the bad,” said Amos, as we drove back to town in his old pickup. “At least, that’s what it done to me. Drop at a time. Don’t know how it all works, really. Only that it does—for some.”

Photo Credit (p 240): bpk Bildagentur / LWL-Museum für Kunst und Kultur, Muenster, Westphalia, Germany / Sabine Ahlbrand-Dornseif / Art Resource, NY

N
NW
NE
W
E
SW
ES
S

BROTHER GAINES

BOB GAINES came out of the late 1970s SoCal sports machine as a skilled long jumper and all-state running back. Burly Bob looked more Clydesdale than quarter horse and had hair all over his body, except on his head (bald as an egg by 30). From the day he first dropped in from Manhattan Beach and onto the grainy rock out at Joshua Tree National Park, Brother Gaines (his nicknames exceeded a hundred) remained a relentless pioneer and a kind of Mr. Chips to his peers and for the many climbers who followed. Bob climbed "over one million routes" (including countless first ascents) in a forty-year, still on-going career, and you'd often hear his name in conversation. Wild rumors and droll slander rolled Bob's way like the Euphrates in flood; most were sideways expressions of the love and admiration we all felt for the mountaineer. Wherever he went, Bob was The Man, showing a maturity and solidness most of us lacked, and which made Bob an excellent guide. His Vertical Adventures Rock Climbing School is one of the best in the country.

Part of our curiosity about Brother Gaines derived from his favored venue—slab climbing, scaling less-than-vertical "slabs" and rock faces via friction, hand, and footholds, often thin as a dime and sharp as razors. Burley Bob belonged on the strenuous cracks, where a climber of his heft and influence can put those muscles to use. So why was Capitol Gaines (always a shrewd businessman) cocking around on arty slabs, where finesse, balance, and deft movement are keys to the castle? Nonetheless, Bob became such a slab maestro he looked like a freight train dancing and skipping on the track. Lynn Hill, many time

World Cup sport climbing champion, insisted Barnacle Bob and the slab were probably dating. Others witnessed Bald Bob on the bald faces and said he deserved his own bobblehead doll, that Brother Gaines was the Brother Gaines of slab climbing.

Bob ranked among the most prolific climbers in America, but his CV reads small compared to his status in popular lore. Over time—eating breakfast, changing a tire, or say, toughing out a marathon drive—someone might ask, "How does one acquire such top-drawer polish as Colonel Gaines?" Such random asides grew into ritual. In the tightest jam, the question was: What would Sheriff Gaines do? He gave the best of us someone to live up to. But the legend of Deacon Gaines drew less from his prowess and more from his character, most noticeably at play with the many clients—often eccentric in the extreme—who he guided for Vertical Adventures.

Take Captain America, whose real name I learned but can't remember. Before social media, Bob promoted his guide service through giving slide shows and demonstrations at outdoors shops scattered around Southern California. One time at Ski Mart, in Newport Beach, as Bob set up his projector, Captain America (Bob's name for him) charged up and pronounced to Bob, "I'm going to climb El Capitan if I have to bash those pie-tons into the rock with my bare hands." The former Marine and now high-roller attorney had never climbed before, and he wanted to attack the most sought-after rock wall on earth. Then traverse to alpine climbing and scale Everest. The Captain had no interest in climbing, per se, only bagging his two dream peaks. He'd pay Mayor Gaines handsomely to get him up El Cap.

After further conversation, and a day trip out to Joshua Tree National Park to learn some basic rope craft, Bob hatched a daring plan. Chairman Gaines, veteran of many El Cap ascents, would lead every pitch on The Nose route, and the Captain would second (follow) on the lead rope, using mechanical ascenders. After a week's instruction and practice in Yosemite Valley, Bob and Captain America jumped straight onto El Capitan.

Captain America was athletic, fit, and fearless, and the climb went exactly as planned, with Bob leading every pitch. After three days, the team arrived at the small bivouac ledge at Camp 6, 2,400 feet up the cliffside. The Captain's spirits, and his person, were sky-high. The summit loomed scarcely 500 feet above. They had passed several parties during their ascent, and each had looked curiously at the second man on Brother Gaines' line, with his glossy red helmet, white pants, blue suede Robbins boots and American flag t-shirt. All of his slings were red, white, or blue. Each item of hardware (Captain American had bought an entire new wall rack for the climb) was painted the same colors. But when a low-flying rescue chopper whirred into the valley 'round about sunset, the thumping rotor blades flashed Captain America back to his darkest days, as a Special Forces grunt in Vietnam. Hunkered on their meager ledge, gripped in a fugue state, the Leatherneck recounted the atrocities he had witnessed, and had carried out himself, so heinous that thirty years later Bob cringes to recall, and will never repeat. Captain

American fell asleep with his teeth clenched, but woke the next morning charged for battle.

They gained the summit at noon, and Captain America declared it his greatest victory. He'd finally climbed above it all. But sadly, not for long. Several years later, Captain America, surely the first non-climber to ever "climb" El Cap, was decapitated while street racing his Turbo Porsche in Topanga Canyon, in the winding hills above Malibu.

Bob's list of quirky clients is long, and legion are the stories of their adventures together, mostly out at Joshua Tree. Like the singular case of "Professor X," a retired physics prof whom Bob first guided on his 55th birthday. Every Monday, Bob went on to guide the prof up the climbs of his choice, often above his pay scale, and often requiring Brother Gaines to winch the corn-fed scientist up the cliff with main force, sometimes constructing a pulley system for the lift. This arrangement continued for thirty years, till Professor X was so old and feeble he had to lean on Bob's shoulder to manage the short hike to the crag. Bob would wrangle him into his harness, rope him in, and would always get the doctor up an approach slab, or even a small boulder. There the team could silently celebrate their victory, gazing across empty desert till the time came to get his client down and into his hiking shoes for the short march back to the car.

Or Cynthia, a retired healthcare worker and raging bipolar who had a "date" with Brother Gaines (a happily married man) every Thursday, when Bob would string a top rope (wherein the rope runs up a short cliff to an anchor on top, then back to the ground, where Brother

Gaines could orchestrate the ascent). Cynthia would scrabble up maybe 10 feet, freak out, and lower back to the ground. She'd stamp her feet and rant fulsomely till she caught a second wind. The she'd creep over the slab once more, swearing like a sailor, gaining a precious few feet on her previous high point. Then back to the deck to unleash the furies. Then back on the slab, and wash and repeat till Bob had coached her up the climb, rarely more than 50 feet high. They'd often stay out till sunset which, out at Joshua, arrives with dazzling palettes of color and sky. Cynthia was often moved by this display, the desert's deep succor and the sure hand of Robert Cornelius Gaines, who held the fort for twenty-five years running, for his client to let off sufficient steam to drive back into the world and function, dreaming about her next date with her guide.

For these three and countless other clients, Brother Gaines gave them what they wanted, and exactly what they needed: the avuncular mentoring of an actual adult, whose generous spirit allowed a critical reset to a world decaying around them. No matter his audience, Bob remained the same unassuming person, in sun and rain and in the dark. Bob became a legendary figure for his countless first ascents, but he held far greater stature in simple reality than the legend he earned from the climbs he bagged, or the inflated tales we loved to fashion around him.

Back when Bob had a beard and ruled the rock, circa 2000, a dozen of us found ourselves huddled around a campfire in County Park, close by Tahquitz Rock. We'd killed all the booze, heads were nodding, and all eyes stared at the fire.

"I hate it when people compare Brother Gaines to Jesus," said my friend, Sara Gould. "I mean, he's great and all, but he's no Brother Gaines."

N
NW
NE
W
E
SW
ES
S

RIPCORD

YOSEMITE VALLEY. Dawn. Mike Lechlinski and I are just stirring in our hammocks, lashed high on the granite face of El Capitan, when a whooshing sound shatters the silence. Louder, closer, building to a roar. Rockfall. Heading right for us: we're dead. I instinctively brace for impact as two BASE jumpers streak over our heads at 120 miles per hour. It seems impossible that two falling bodies can make such terrifying, ear-splitting racket, like God is ripping the sky in half with his bare hands. We scream, craning our heads from our hammocks, our eyes following the jumpers plunging into the void. Their arms dovetail back as they track away from the cliff. The pop of their chutes fires up the wall like shotgun blasts. They swoop over treetops and land 50 feet into the meadow as a beater station wagon screeches to a stop on the loop road. The jumpers bundle their canopies, jog over, and dive into the beater, which quickly drives off. This last bit looks sped up, like a Roadrunner cartoon. If the rangers catch them in the act, they're going to jail. We howl because we're still there, still alive.

"I think I pissed myself," says Mike. On a scale of one to a shitload, this sixty-second lark is off the chart.

In 1984, the adventure world caught fire and every serious player tried to blaze like hell. From our first sorties free climbing big walls to jungleering across Oceania, the mantra never changed: capture the burning flag. Our cousins in big wave surfing, kayaking, cave diving, and mountain biking were also charging hard, and we watched our group fever trigger the adventure-sport revolution. And the most visually dramatic show of them all was BASE jumping, the acronym for parachuting from a Building, Antenna, Span (bridge), and the Earth (cliffs).

A couple years after my close encounter on El Cap, I needed something bold to gain traction in the TV business, where I hoped to quickly score the trophy girls and crazy money. I was two months out of school, with a fistful of so-what degrees and a junker Volkswagen Beetle, determined to leave Yosemite behind. But secretly I didn't so much wave at the train as grab for it, afraid of getting left behind.

British talk show maven and future Richard Nixon interviewer, David Frost, had a boutique production house with Sunset Boulevard offices. I hired on as a writer and associate producer, knowing zero about the television racket. The salary didn't dazzle but my future glowed. We had several hour-long *Guinness Book of World Records* specials that we needed to style out with electrifying content. Previous episodes featured a dull parade of magicians, carnivorous spiders, and an English mastiff named Claudius, the world's largest dog. I promised to hose out the dog shit, clean up the show, and boost the numbers. I knew going in that staging world-class adventures for television was sketchy, but so what. I was handy with danger and eager to debut BASE jumping on primetime national television. The plan felt like money. That left the tricky bit: collaring someone to do the jumping.

My immediate boss, Ian, smooth, sardonic, and classically educated at Eton, favored exciting acts. BASE jumping was one of several adventure pursuits, each riskier than the last, that I'd scribbled onto our dance card, and which the network, indemnified of responsibility, could promote to the moon. Ratings were everything, but in Jack Daniels moments Ian sometimes asked, "We're not going to get anyone killed doing this, are we?"

"Not if I can help it," I'd say.

The stars aligned and, in late June, I flew to London and joined Carl Boenish and his wife, Jean. Carl, 43, later dubbed "the father of BASE jumping," was a free-fall cinematographer who, in the 1970s, had filmed the inaugural jumps from El Capitan, plus many other "first exits" off high-rise buildings, antennas, and bridges. For sheer burn and ebullience, Carl had few peers. Jean, nineteen years Carl's junior, brainy, wholesome, and distant as polar ice, lived her life in a language I didn't understand.

From London, Carl, Jean, and I flew to Oslo. The Norwegian airlines had gone on strike, so we packed six duffel bags into a rental station wagon and headed for the Troll Peaks in the Romsdalen valley, eight hours north. The narrow road meandered through still green valleys, dark as tourmaline, laced with alpine streams and glinting under the midnight sun. We stopped for beers at an inn (ginger ale for the Boenishes, who took no liquor), and I marveled at the year, 1509, chiseled on the stone hearth. Finally, we crept into the sleepy town of Åndalsnes, surrounded by misty cliffs, including the Trollveggen, Europe's tallest vertical rock face, a brooding gneiss hulk featuring several notorious rock climbs and the proposed site for our world-record BASE jump. "Built when the mountain was built," folklore says of Åndalsnes.

Carl and I breakfasted on pickled cod, peanut butter, and black coffee, and zigzagged up a steep road to the highest path and set out on a leg-busting trudge for Trollveggen's summit. We were joined by Fred Husoy, a young local, among the finest adventure climbers in Europe, who knew the Troll massif by heart—critical in locating our jump site. We shouldered packs and trudged over shifty moraines toward a snowy col.

The first few miles climbed a glacial plateau, broken occasionally by lichen-flecked boulders and gray snow drifts that never melted, carved by wind into gargoyles and labyrinths. The lunar emptiness hadn't changed in a billion years, and held the silence of the dead when the wind died down. It was so big and so blinding that even the birds felt lost in it, how they'd break the stillness and cry out. An elegiac keening that climbed to the ridgeline and broke. Another bird would answer. But the birds were not lonesome for each other. It was bigger than that.

From the moment we'd hit the trail, Carl hiked so slowly that I finally took his pack; but halfway over the big white plane, he once more had fallen well behind. Fred pulled on his raincoat against the drizzle, warning we had to hike faster or get blown off the mountain by afternoon storms. We slogged ankle-deep through a snowfield. When Carl caught up, wet clouds draped everything. No coaxing could make him hike faster. A little stone hut twenty minutes shy of the summit ridge offered a welcome roof from the shower. Carl limped in, collapsed, and pulled up a pant leg. Fred and I stared. Right above the ankle, Carl's femur took a shocking jag, as if he'd snapped it in half and the bone had healed inches off plumb. I felt small and mean to have pushed him. How did a person hike at all with a leg like that?

"Jesus. When did that happen?" I asked. He'd shattered his leg in a hang-gliding accident several years back, said Carl, who clenched his way through a wonky exposition on natural healing.

"I don't know, Carl," I said. "A bone doc could surely fix that. It's hideous." Carl swished the air with his hand. Who needed doctors when God Almighty would set things right? His fingers trembled as he pulled up his sock. It felt incredible and reckless to stake my future on a man living off stardust and voodoo.

A week before, we'd organized the venture at Carl's house in Hawthorne, a small, L.A. suburb. From the moment I stepped through the door, Jean eyed me with steely reckoning, as though if she glanced away I might pilfer the china. Her clothes looked Mennonite-plain, the house, immaculate, all cups and chairs and handcuffs in their place. Nothing admitted she and Carl dove off cliffs for a living. As Carl raked through his garage, overflowing with gear, he'd bloviate about St. Peter, Coco Joe, or whoever. Without warning, Carl would dash to his piano and butcher some Brahms or Brubeck, then jump back into conversation, randomly ranging from electrical engineering to terracotta sculpture to trampolines and particle physics, galvanized by a screwy amalgam of new age doctrine and personal revelations. Often, he would heave all this out in the same sprawling rant. Ian thought he'd dropped acid. But Carl laughed so loud and burned so hot I found myself giddy by the inspired way he met the world. We lived in different keys, but we both craved the intimacy of risk. And in the fellowship of adventurers, folks like Carl Boenish drove the bus.

Outside our little stone hut in the Troll Peaks, the shower slacked off and we continued over snowy slabs toward the mile-long summit ridge, all dark clefts, precarious boxcar blocks, and pinnacles digging into the sky, so twisted and multidimensional, M.C. Escher couldn't have drawn it in his dreams. The wall dropped 6,000 feet directly off the ridge and into the Trondheim valley. The rubbly slabs angled down behind us to the high glacial plateau, where perpetual snow framed a tiny lake glowing aquamarine. Black-and-white clouds gathered, masking the ridge, cutting visibility to several hundred feet and making it difficult to navigate. Without Fred's knowledge of the labyrinthine summit backbone, we would have wandered blind. The clouds parted and we lay belly-down on the brink, sticking our heads out over the immediate, sucking drop. Carl rubbed his leg, laughed, grimaced, and laid out his requirements.

The wall directly beneath his launch must overhang for hundreds of feet, he said, long enough for a plunging BASE jumper to reach near-terminal velocity. Only at top speed, when the air became thick as water, could his layout positioning create enough horizontal draft to track and fly out and away from the wall (the now-ubiquitous wingsuit wouldn't be invented for another dozen years) to pop the chute, as Mike and I had witnessed on El Capitan. The new parachutes didn't simply drop vertically, but sported a three-to-one glide ratio—three feet forward for one foot down. But twisted lines could sometimes deploy a chute backwards, wrenching the jumper around and into the cliff.

"Here, that would be fatal," said Carl with buggy eyes, peering back over the lip.

The most prominent spires along the ridgeline were named after chess pieces. Out left loomed The Castle, a striking, 200-foot-high spire canting off the brink like the Tower of Pisa. An exit from the summit, hanging out over oblivion like that, had to be safer than leaping straight off the summit ridge, making it an obvious feature to scout.

Carl hung back as Fred and I tied on a rope and scrambled up the water-logged Castle to the top—a flat and shattered parapet, perfect to start our rock tests. We wobbled a chair-sized boulder over to the lip and shoved it off. Five, six . . . *Bam*—a sound like mortar fire. Debris rattled down for ages.

"No good," said Carl, yelling from the ridgeline. "Way too soon to impact." We tried again. This time, I leaned over the lip and watched a second rock whiz downward, swallowed in fog 300 feet below. Three, four . . . *Bam!* My head snapped up. There had to be jutting ledges mere feet below the fog line. We shoved off more rocks and kept hearing the immediate, violent impact of stone on stone. "Forget it," Carl yelled. "The Castle will never do. It'd be crazy." The flinty smell of shattered rock wafted up as Fred and I rappelled off the pinnacle and joined Carl.

For another hour we continued with the rock tests, at successive points along the rubbly brink. Trundling rocks off most any other cliff could kill people. Not there. Any climbers on the wall and we'd have known about them. And below the towering upper wall spilled a massive, low-angled slab, terminating in a sprawling moraine field where nobody but climbers had reason to go. The menace, though huge, was strictly our own. All around us loomed forces and forms so elemental they had never organized into life, so nothing native to this place could even die. But we could. That's what made it so heady to try and sort this out. But each rock we shouldered off dashed the wall within seconds. Lightning cracked off the lower ridge and we ran for the valley. Carl hobbled behind.

Norwegians are a handsome race, normally demure, until you pull the cork on Friday afternoon and the *dritt* hits the *vifte*. That night, all the young locals in town crammed into the pub in the hotel's basement, where we drank Frydenlund like mad, chased it with beer, and danced to The Who. Several gallons in, a tall brunette with a stylish bob grabbed a handful of my shirt. She acted more curious than courageous, and couldn't find the words. So I trotted out the one Norwegian phrase I had memorized from a handbook in my room: "*Hvorkanjegkjøpe en vikinghjelm*?" (Where can I purchase a Viking helmet?)

"Are you a Viking?" she asked in flawless English. I said I'd try to be one for her, and she said, "You will marry me." That night I saw eternity and it looked like this: a girl and a boy dancing in a crowd on an unswept floor in a bar on a thousand-year-old street.

Aud came from the next town over, and worked some dreary retail job in Åndalsnes during summer break from nursing school. We spent our free time together, and I learned there are moments where nothing is so grim as being alone. I usually went it alone, a shark who survived by staying in motion. Until Aud drew the restlessness from me like a thorn, and light leaked through a soul cracked open. Over the next month, as we got the jump site dialed and waited for good weather, I was either with Aud or imagining her.

The next day, as Carl recovered in his hotel room, Fred and I slogged back to the summit ridge for our first of many recons, trying to locate a viable launch site. The existing world's longest BASE jump, first established three years before, exited the ridge well east and some 400 feet lower than the Castle. That left us to scour the chaotic, quarter-mile-long ridge between The Castle and the old site—a confusing task for sure. Over the following weeks, when we weren't kicking around the Trollveggen's cloudy ramparts, Fred and I would snag Aud and go bouldering on huge, mossy erratics, or hike up spectacular peaks or along jagged ridges snaking through the sky. I was 26;

Fred and Aud were in their early 20s, all of us novice adults, searching for where we fit into the world. For a weightless moment, we shared an enchantment. Twice more, Fred and I explored the summit ridge, ever dashed by hailstorms.

The rain, meanwhile, kept washing our budget into the talus, and my inability to locate a jump site was wearing us out. Norway completed our production schedule, and the crew looked toward holidays in Paris, the Greek Islands, or home. We had to get this done. On the ninth scout, after a nasty piece of scrambling and several tension traverses on crappy rock, we located the highest possible exit from the ridge: The Bishop, to use the old chess name. But again, we got weathered off before we made our rock tests. We returned early the next day and, lucky for us, the sky shone all blue distance, the entire ridge fantastically visible and spilling down on both sides for miles. After weeks spent wandering about in the fog, it felt like a vision from the Bible, the entire rambling cordillera unmasked before us. We definitely were on the apex, walking unroped on an anvil-flat, 10-by-50-foot ledge that terminated in an abyss as sudden and arresting as the lip of the Grand Canyon. If the rock tests checked out, we were halfway home. The easy half.

I lashed myself taut to two separate lines, bent over the drop, and lobbed off a bowling-ball-sized rock while Fred timed the free fall. The rock accelerated ferociously and dropped clean from sight. Twelve, thirteen . . . I glanced over at Fred and smiled. This could be it. Seventeen, eighteen . . . *BANG*! A faint puff of white smoke appeared thousands of feet below. That rock had just free-fallen three quarters of a mile. No question, The Bishop was our record site. Fred pointed out the original launch spot (or exit site), still far left and 300-something feet below. I chucked another rock and we watched it shrink to a pea and burst like a sneeze near the base, the echo volleying up from the amphitheater. I tried to imagine strapping on a chute and plunging off, but couldn't. And I couldn't yet imagine ever climbing this towering heap.

From a distance, Trollveggen looked classic, a 2,000-foot-high talus slope topped by a 3,600-foot rock wall. At its steepest, the summit ridge overhung the base by 160 feet. Up close, however, the greatest rock wall in Europe was all fractured statuary, a vertical rubble pile top to bottom. And so utterly, unspeakably *other*, neither alive nor dead. It simply was, somehow, and it spooked me more by the day and the week.

We ascended our fixed rope, reversed the traverse and, as the first raindrops fell, Fred and I hoofed it to the valley with the good news.

For the next five days, Aud, Fred, and I stayed glued to the Oslo news channel, frequently stepping outside and glancing through thundershowers for some providential patch of blue. Mostly we milled around the production HQ in the hotel basement, living off chocolate scones and espresso. Helicopters stood on standby, film cameras were loaded, every angle reckoned, logistics planned to the minute. Meanwhile, journalists throughout Scandinavia streamed into Åndalsnes. The local paper ran full-page spreads in a town where the breaking news trended toward a farmer hooking a record lunker in a secret stream. When approached and pried at, Carl would laugh and let fly his exotic babbling as journalists nodded and smiled but took no notes. Finally, Jean—normally so laconic she might have been mute—would answer with several cold facts and figures.

A celebrated Oslo stringer, newly arrived, cited previous BASE jumping accidents and questioned something that had every official chewing their nails. As starry-eyed admirers gathered to touch Carl's jumpsuit, she all but screamed that the emperor had no clothes. The glossy hype and big money spent was nothing but a made-for-TV flim-flam in the service of a maniac who, by the sound of him, had flunked kindergarten and had little regard for his own safety. The worry on her face and edge in her words betrayed her annoyance that The Jump had a gravity even she couldn't escape. None of this was simple.

We slunk around. Rain fell in sheets. Tension mounted. With all the media hoopla, all the delays, each emerging detail raised the story's sails sky-high. Norwegian television ran nightly updates. The big Oslo station sent a video truck. With a week's momentum, the production took on the pomp and blather of Hollywood—precisely what I'd hoped to avoid.

Several journalists took to quoting Carl directly. The translation to Norwegian vexed ("like Ted Hughes on peyote," Ian suggested), the waiting game somewhat relieved by trying to guess what the hell Carl had said. The sky growled at us. Scandinavia stood by. Each day in limbo meant thousands of dollars lost to feed, liquor, and house the crew. This quickly morphed into an impatience for what required steadfast deliberation. Throughout, the Boenishes were ready to jump. At 8 p.m., July 5, 1984, the weather broke.

Everyone scrambled, desperate to shoot something, even in bad light. In two hours, cameramen choppered into position. The helicopter dumped Carl, Jean, Fred, and me into a small notch 40 feet from the launch site on The Bishop. This avoided having to wheedle the Boenishes across the traverses, fitted with fixed ropes, that had given Fred and me fits owing to loose rock. Carl pulled on his flaming red jumpsuit and paced around like someone waiting for the electric chair. Jean began assiduously studying the launch site. I pitched off a rock that whistled into the night. Other rocks followed to verify my estimates, but disclosed another hazard.

"Sure, they drop forever," laughed Carl, "and that's a good thing. But they're never more than ten feet from the wall." That left no margin for error. If they couldn't stick the perfect, horizontal free-fall position, if they carved the air even slightly back-tilted—head higher than feet—they could possibly track backwards. Carl demonstrated with his hands, one hand as the wall, the other for the jumper. When his hands smacked together, Fred and I jumped. Jean, cool as the Romsdal Fjord, rolled more stones toward the lip. The light faded to a gray pall. Far below, the great stone amphitheater swallowed the night.

The radio coughed out: "*Come on, mate, let's get on with it!*" The crew was freezing and the director of photography feared it would quickly get too dark to film.

"Hey," said Carl, lucid as water, "I can't be rushed to jump off this cliff, screaming past those ledges at midnight." I quoted this word-for-word into the radio, and the crew backed off. They'd planned to jump in tandem—Jean first, followed closely by Carl—but for this run-through, Carl chose to huck a solo jump while the cameramen previewed and assessed the angles. The sun, at the wee hours, was too dim for full glory, but a practice jump could help the cameramen dial in the details. The sky, though darkening, remained clear and flawless so, with some luck, the good weather might hold. After Carl's trial jump, we'd resume in a few hours, when full light returned.

Carl strapped on his parachute and I tried to capture his kinetic energy on film. But I couldn't pull a focus in the gloom. I packed away the Ariflex, grabbed a still camera, and turned to the drama before the jump.

"Ten minutes," said Carl, bug-eyed, jaw working, hands fidgety. Jean helped Carl with the last straps. Cued by days of front-page spreads, the road below swarmed with cars and people, headlights winking in 1 a.m. gloom.

"Five minutes," said Carl.

He pulled some streamers from his pack. Leaning off the ropes, I lobbed them off. No wind. They fell straight toward the base, shrinking to a blur. Everything looked *go*.

"One minute," said Carl, his voice high and tight. He cinched his helmet and slid twitching fingers into white gloves. I pitched off a final rock and Carl tracked it, visualizing his line.

"Fifteen seconds."

Carl unclipped the rope and stepped over to the lip. Horns sounded below. I was tied off to several ropes, my feet on the edge, with a panoramic view for the ages.

Carl's shoes tapped like a rhythm machine, eyes unfocused. He started his countdown, which Fred mimicked into the radio: "Four, three, two, one!" And he was off. Watching someone jump straight off a cliff like this is so counterintuitive to a climber's instincts that Carl might as well have jumped into the next world. The void swallowed him alive, his streaking form more easily imagined than described. The air froze in my chest.

After a few seconds, Carl's arms went out to stabilize, his legs bending and straightening while his jumpsuit whipped like a flag. With roaring speed, Carl passed several ledges with 10 feet to spare, body whooshing, ripping the air with a violent report. After 1,000 feet, his arms snapped to his sides as he flew horizontally away from the wall, tracking 50, 100, 150 feet, at 120 miles per hour, a swooping red dot. Thirteen seconds, fourteen, fifteen . . . *Pop*! His yellow chute unfurled big as a circus tent, and he glided down, over the slab and moraine field to the meadow. The picture-perfect jump.

Fred and I crabbed back from the lip, gaped at each other, and howled. Some called Carl an idiot for risking his life over something that didn't matter; but we'd just watched him rogue fear with imagination, and dive into the unknown. And if that doesn't matter, nothing much does.

Back at the hotel at three-thirty a.m., the chaotic crews,

gnashing producers, frantic journalists, film loaders, battery chargers, pilots, and hangers-on, all guzzled espresso and ducked out to check for clouds, everyone anxious to film the jump and clear out. A chartered jet sat gassed and awaiting the crew once we finished filming, hopefully by noon. At four a.m., I laid down with Aud for a short nap, but couldn't settle for all the caffeine and apprehension.

At six a.m., two helicopters ground up through Persian blue skies and deposited us on The Bishop. Half an hour later, after some rock tests, and rechecking their rigs, the laces on their shoes, the film and batteries in their helmet-mounted cameras, Jean tiptoed to the lip, with Carl inches behind her. I stood five feet away, lashed to a rope, toes curled over the brink, shouldering a 16 mm film camera. 100 feet straight out in space, the helicopter yawed and hovered like a dragonfly. Fred gave the order to roll cameras. The Boenishes stepped off the lip and dropped into the void. Jean later wrote:

Eyes fixed on the horizon, I raise my arms into a good exit position. Then from behind, 'Three! Two! One!' For an instant my eyes dart down to reaffirm one solid step before the open air. Go! One lunging step forward and I'm off, Carl right on my heels. Freedom! Silence accelerates into the rushing sound as my body rolls forward. I quickly realize that the last downward glance has been an indulgence now taking its toll, for I roll past the prone into a head-down dive, which takes me too close to the wall. The first ledge is rushing towards me as I strain to keep from flipping over onto my back.

Through the viewfinder I watched Jean dive-bomb and

slowly cant over onto her back. I panicked and ripped away the camera as she plummeted, her toes nearly brushing the first ledge.

"Holy shit!" Fred yelled.

Jean somehow arched back to prone, her hands came back, and the duo swooped away from the wall, shrinking to colorful specks, still flying, 200 feet out, still free-falling. Their training, from thousands of skydives and hundreds of BASE jumps, steered them down the face. But watching the pair, as they streaked toward hungry boulders, stopped my heart.

"Pull the chute!" I screamed. Sixteen seconds, seventeen: *POP! POP!* A world record, no injuries. Cameramen raved over the radios. Newsmen and bystanders swarmed the Boenishes after their pinpoint landing. The world toppled off our shoulders.

Fred and I were done, and drained. Nothing but smiles, chocolate strawberries, and champagne back at the hotel. Ian and I both thought we had a shot at an Emmy with this one, and my career in television glowed. Aside from the delays, the jump had gone exactly as planned, but the crew scrambled to pack and leave on the charter. Ian was so worried about an accident that he rushed to clear out lest something happen retroactively. That afternoon the charter jetted for London, and those left behind, including half the kids in Åndalsnes, moved to the bar in the hotel basement, where several storylines began to converge. I could never have guessed where this junket was about to take us.

A Norwegian named Stein Gabrielsen and his fellow countryman Eric (last name unknown) had arrived in Åndalsnes only hours before. I met them in the bar, thinking they were another two Euro BASE jumpers drawn there by the big news, now splashed across Europe. In fact, while Fred, Carl, and I had begun scouting Trollveggen's summit ridge, Stein and Eric (both working in America, and unaware of our plans) had purchased one-way tickets to Norway to attempt the world-record jump off the Troll Wall, something they'd planned for three years. They would have gotten the record, too, except they'd gone on a ten-day bender the moment they met with friends in Oslo. When a girl showed Stein the newspaper story about how Carl and Jean were already in Åndalsnes, waiting for the clouds to lift, he and Eric bolted directly, arriving in town late that evening.

They walked to the base of the Troll Wall, still glowing under the midnight sun, both men eager to scope out their record site. That's where they met "a drunk old Norwegian dude" who pointed at the dark cliffs and said, "That is the Devil's mountain." They walked back to town and spent their last krone on beer at the pub, where several dozen of us were finishing our wrap party, a Hollywood tradition. I remained the final holdover from the American production crew, there to settle accounts and hang with Aud. Stein and Eric, both flat broke, joined the bash only to learn the Boenishes had scooped them by a few hours. At best, they might repeat the record—the adventure-sports version of an asphalt cigar. Their consolation was the $500 of production money I had left to blow on booze.

"Eric and I found Carl," said Stein, "congratulated him, and asked about his launch site." Carl said he jumped from The Bishop. Stein had surveyed the ridge and believed The Castle stood higher. "Check a chess set," said Carl. "The Bishop is always taller than The Castle." "Either way," said Stein, "Eric and I are jumping The Castle tomorrow."

"Carl became visibly nervous," Stein later wrote, "and suggested we meet at their hotel for breakfast next morning, around ten a.m. Then we could go jump together." A free meal sounded good, so Stein and Eric agreed. We closed the bar and half-mashed on Aquavit; Aud and I staggered to her apartment and I passed out for twelve hours.

The following morning, Stein and Eric met Jean at the hotel. Jean said Carl was in town, arranging their travel back to the States, and she invited the pair to breakfast. An hour passed and still no Carl. Jean kept glancing at her watch, out at the driveway, back at the map of Trollveggen hanging on the wall. Jean said she was sorry. She'd deceived them. Carl had been afraid they would usurp his record (as The Castle is higher on the ridgeline than Carl and Jean's launch site on The Bishop), so he'd left at sunrise to go jump The Castle. Jean figured he had already jumped and was at the landing field, waiting for a ride. She suggested Stein and Eric take the rental Volvo, snag Carl, and head back up to The Castle for round two. Jean needed to pack. Stein and Eric had gotten snookered and sent to fetch the culprit. One can imagine their conversation as they drove to the landing zone in the big meadow, to talk things through with Carl Boenish.

Back at Aud's apartment, I sorted gear for a one-day, racehorse ascent of the Troll Wall. I'd changed my mind a hundred times, but couldn't blow off Europe's biggest cliff when it was right down the road. A quick rap on Aud's door. It flew open and Fred rushed in.

"Carl's been in an accident," he said, "and it looks bad." A car accident? "No," said Fred. Early that morning, Carl had hiked back up to Trollveggen and jumped off The Castle. That couldn't be right. After the last two days tromping around, Carl would be resting his bum leg for sure. Our production had caused such a stir that, for going on a week, jumpers like Stein and Eric continued streaming in from Sweden, Iceland, Denmark, and beyond. Any accident was theirs, I said, not Carl's. Fred shook his head. Carl had enlisted two teenage brothers, both local climbers, to hike him up. One, Arnstein Myskja, had witnessed Carl's accident and stood there next to Fred, trembling in his boots.

Ten minutes later, I was dashing across peat bogs, seeking a vantage point with the lower Troll Wall in clear view. I frantically glassed the lower face, nearly a mile away, finally spotting Carl's big yellow parachute, unfurled and breeze-blown on a shaded terrace near the base.

"Goddamn it, Carl. Get up . . . signal . . ." The canopy billowed gently from the updraft. "Carl!"

Fred arrived and put a hand on my shoulder. Carl hadn't

moved. I followed Fred to a grassy field surrounding the grand manor of an expatriate British lord. A pall tumbled from gray clouds as the media streamed in, occasionally stealing glances our way. My center could not hold much longer.

The police chief arrived and I couldn't meet his eyes when I told him I'd spotted Carl on a ledge near the base. The part about no movement ended our conversation. I didn't have the courage to call Jean, but the chief did. Barely. Tears flowed from his eyes though his voice remained calm and stoic. I will never forget his face as he talked with Jean.

"I . . . regret to inform you that your husband has been in an accident, and it doesn't look good." This last detail took enormous bravery to admit. Jean's voice sounded eerily detached over the speaker phone, soberly seeking details as every soul in Åndalsnes bore the chaos on her behalf. I stormed outside and pulled on my harness. Nobody knew if Carl was dead, or even seriously injured, and I yelled as much, confronting some with the news. They nodded slowly and shrank away, huddling under trees, waiting.

The *whop, whop* of the giant military rescue chopper thundered up the valley. It landed in a clearing, arching trees, buckling photographers, scaring all with its powerful thumping. Fred went and I stayed behind, shivering in my t-shirt and glaring up into the rain. Aud came over but I couldn't talk or look at her. I thought about nothing, vaguely hearing the chopper's hammering pitch in the distance. It set down and the crew filed out, staring at the ground. Fred walked over, his face hard as stone. Six photographers clicked shots as we fled back to the lord's house.

As a free citizen, Carl could do as he pleased, but The Castle? I yelled. Carl himself had called the site crazy. The doctor, little more than thirty years old, requested that I go aboard to identify the body. "For what?" I begged. The doctor stared at the floor. The ordeal was far from over, and spared nobody. I felt like the Ugly American who had barged into a quiet little town with a small army and a wad of television money and broke every rule and every heart in the place.

We walked through wet, knee-high grass toward the ship. Amber light glinted off new puddles. How dare beauty show itself when Carl was dead? We moved through the chopper's huge rear hold and back to Carl's body, looking as though he'd laid down to get a load off that leg. No sign of regret on his face. The young doctor and I stood there, mourning a life cut in half, gazing from death as if unhurt. But he'd screamed a music too high to scale, and the cold mountain got him. The distance Carl had tracked away from us brought back the birds and their keening, high on the glacial plateau.

I joined the crowd gathering on the grassy field, everyone gazing confusedly at each other. Someone had to know why and how come. We watched the coroner and two policemen heft Carl's black-bagged body into a white van and roll off into the mist. It felt criminal to leave it at that; but Carl could not die again. That was all. The end.

Fred and I silently drove to Aud's place and I wandered

in a traceless land. Even Aud couldn't help me now. Why had Carl jumped from The Castle? I'd never felt such helpless confusion, and could have killed Carl a second time.

That evening I went and found Arnstein who, along with his younger brother, had guided Carl that morning. It had taken them nearly five hours to short-rope (drag by a tethered line) Carl over the glacial plateau and up to the top of The Castle. Carl conducted rock tests and, in seconds, as before, they smashed off outcroppings jutting directly into the flight path. But Carl was determined to go. Arnstein grabbed his camera. As he described to me and others, Carl was dead the moment he launched off the lip, or tried to. On his last exit step, he stumbled and, unable to push off and get some little separation from the wall, he frantically tossed out his pilot chute. With so little airspeed, it lazily fluttered up, slowly pulling his main chute from the pack. One side of the chute's chambers filled with air and flew forward. With one side deflated, the inflated side wrenched the canopy sharply, whipping Carl around and into the cliff.

He continued tumbling, said Arnstein, his lines and the canopy spooling around him like a cocoon. 5,000 feet later, Carl's tightly wound body impacted the lower slab "and bounced thirty feet in the air like a basketball." Arnstein was so sickened by what he'd just shot on his Nikon that he yanked the film from the roll and tossed it into the void, so the images of Carl's last moments were lost forever.

A few days later, Jean hired several local climbers to

hike her up to The Castle, where she checked the site firsthand and did what a wife does where her husband has died. Then she traversed the ridge to the original, 1981 launch site, jumped off and touched down for a perfect meadow landing.

I couldn't sit and kept pacing around Aud's tiny apartment. For several weeks, I'd agonized over leaving Norway without her—a puzzling concern for a nomad like me. But life kept shifting. TV work stretched off like a cargo cult runway, inviting a rich future to appear. Then Carl crash-landed and it felt likely I was one and done with production work. Staring at the white stucco walls in Aud's matchbox, I couldn't see any future at all. I don't recall saying goodbye to Aud and Fred, but I must have. I only remember driving through the dark dawn shadow of Troll Wall, heading for the airport in Molde, the giant cliff felt but unseen for all the clouds and rain.

Over the following decades, Carl and Jean's Norway jump became a seminal event in BASE jumping's short history. Several magazines ran feature articles on the couple, but they'd taken a novelist's wand to Carl's accident, and I couldn't read them through. I wasn't surprised when a producer called about a feature-length documentary on Carl, now in production, and asked if I might fly over to Åndalsnes and do an interview. Time had worked the sharpest edges off Carl's death, and a trip to

Europe sounded excellent. I found myself back in Norway a few months later.

The Trondheim Valley, and that towering junker, Trollveggen, were far more daunting than I remembered—which wasn't much. Åndalsnes had modernized but still resembled a sub-burg of Camelot. My feel for the place had gone. Thirty years can blunt the sharpest memories. Mix in drink, work, a failed marriage, and it's a miracle I remember anything. Fred and I reunited and immediately went bouldering at the old haunts—the mushy fields and cow pies, the scabby orange lichen on the rock, gaping up at the monstrous Troll Wall, "doing the joking" as we floundered on short climbs we'd once hiked with ease. The memories stirred. I talked to Aud on the phone and her voice pulled me back. But I still felt lost as the birds on the glacial plateau.

The next day, I met the film crew at a grassy campground directly beneath Trollveggen, rearing a mile beyond us. The director was a jocular young woman from Los Angeles, with heaps of passionate intensity. The director of photography, a pondering Swede, would tuck an entire tin of snuff behind his lower lip and pace, mulling the next shot and spewing vile brown pools like the spoor of a wounded elk. The two went back and forth about the lighting, arguing like they meant it, so I didn't sit for the interview till around noon. It started raining.

They'd paid handsomely to fly me there, so I felt obliged to drop into deep thoughts and important feelings. But I couldn't peel off my armor. The director bore in. As I recounted the details, and Carl's eccentric stoke and fearlessness, the top layer didn't so much wear thin as sludge from far below came bubbling up. Yet I spoke without color, owing to the gray way the past came back to me. The questions moved to The Castle, and the rescue chopper. Standing in a drizzle and glaring up, I slammed through the looking glass.

For several minutes I said nothing, sinking lower in my chair. The rain beat down and we stopped filming. I didn't move. The director pulled a blanket over my shoulders. For an instant, I could see my life with jarring clarity as it ran from that July day in Åndalsnes, three decades before, and how my native love for cinematic narratives never made it off that rescue chopper. The part of me that can actually write was wedged like an iron strut between then and now as I continued to muddle along in productions I didn't believe in, without passion or inspiration, an also-ran in an industry made for me—a selfish take on "The Jump," as they called it, but Carl's death was the ogre who prowled my unconscious, setting me on my screwy course in life.

Over the next half hour, I'm uncertain what I said, but I meant every word—and it was mostly news to me. Then the director asked why I thought Carl had risked a jump that he'd previously called "crazy." For years, this question had lingered over The Jump, adding texture and intrigue to the strangeness of Carl's last words.

As Arnstein had later told Stein Erik Gabrielsen, as Carl stepped toward the edge of The Castle, he abruptly paused and asked, "Do you boys know the Bible?" Wide-eyed and anxious, they said, "Yes, of course." "Remember when the Devil takes Jesus high up onto the temple roof," asked Carl, "and tempts him to cast himself off, for surely the angels will rescue him?" "Yes," Arnstein had said. He knew the story. Carl reached one hand over the other shoulder, patted his parachute, and said, "I don't need angels."

The man who would walk on water and fly through the air—is he closer to God, or possessed, gaslighted by glory, adrenaline, and a lifetime of narrow escapes? Carl turned, took two steps toward the edge and, on the third step, he stumbled.

That night I sat alone in my room, muddling through an old issue of *Granta* I'd nicked from the hotel lobby. For years, I'd stepped on the gas and whoosh—the far side of life was fast approaching. Scrolling back, I could finally sense the penumbra of Aud and I, like perfume on an old pillow. We'd spoken several times and thought it best not to meet in person. When I called and asked her to reconsider, she arrived in the lobby ten minutes later. We stared at each other, dazed to realize that once we'd been young together. I could have ridden that feeling into the ground. Instead, I powered up my laptop and showed Aud photos of my two daughters: Marjohny, with all the freckles, and Marianne, a recently minted MD, both stunners because they take after their mother. When Aud's daughter arrived, I was staring at Aud herself—a young woman exuding life the way a lamp gives off light. She looked at me curiously. A man from her mother's past, standing before her and looking at the future. It's all an enchantment.

Stein Gabrielsen and his friend, Eric, had barely arrived in the Romsdalen valley when a local drunkard pointed to Trollveggen and said, "That is the Devil's mountain." Eight hours later, Carl died quoting the Devil tempting Jesus to fly. Eric, a wizard in the air, jumped the Troll Wall three times over the days following Carl's death. On his last jump, Eric logged a thirty-second free-fall with a two-second canopy ride before landing in the rocks, miraculously unhurt. He declined to document the record free-fall because the only way for someone to top it was to bounce. "Get me out of here before I die," he told Stein. Stein quit drinking on the spot and hasn't jumped since.

Eric is currently a healer in Berlin and skydives regularly. Stein runs a small church (Saint Galileo) and teaches kite-surfing in Miami. He still gets occasional flashes of Eric nearly going in during his thirty-second free fall. "For now," he later wrote, "I am content with the knowledge that I am a fool. Every day I thank my angels and pray for wisdom."

In winter, 1989, Arnstein Myskja, the teenage guide who witnessed Carl's last jump, was swept to his death by an avalanche while climbing the Mjelva Gully, rising above the Mjelva Boulder, the moss-covered stone where Fred and I practiced climbing, waiting for the clouds to part on Trollveggen.

Aud is a nurse's supervisor, has two teenaged daughters, and is married to a fellow Norwegian who manages oil platforms in the North Sea.

Fred Husoy went on to climb many new routes in the Trondheim Valley, the Alps, and the Himalayas. He led the local rescue team for many years and, through innovative, often perilous efforts, saved dozens of climbers injured on the Troll Wall. He is married to a doctor and has two sons.

Half a dozen years after The Jump, while parachuting onto a limestone Tepui in the Venezuelan rainforest, Jean Boenish open-fractured her leg, greatly curtailing her BASE jumping career. A common saying in adventure circles is that BASE jumping has killed more people than malaria.

The film about Carl Boenish, called *Sunshine Superman*, earned critical acclaim. Producers felt robbed that it didn't earn the Academy Award for live-action documentary. The director invited me to a private screening shortly after the premiere, thick with industry people, but I left early. It took me three times to finally watch it through.

A few months after returning from Norway, I came tumbling down in a climbing gym, of all places. The first thing I saw when I rolled onto my ass was my tibia jutting from a fist-sized hole in my shin. I spent the next forty-five days in the hospital. One time in the wee hours when I couldn't sleep and the morphine carried me off to the ethers, I gazed down and saw a girl and a boy dancing to The Who in a bar on a thousand-year-old street.

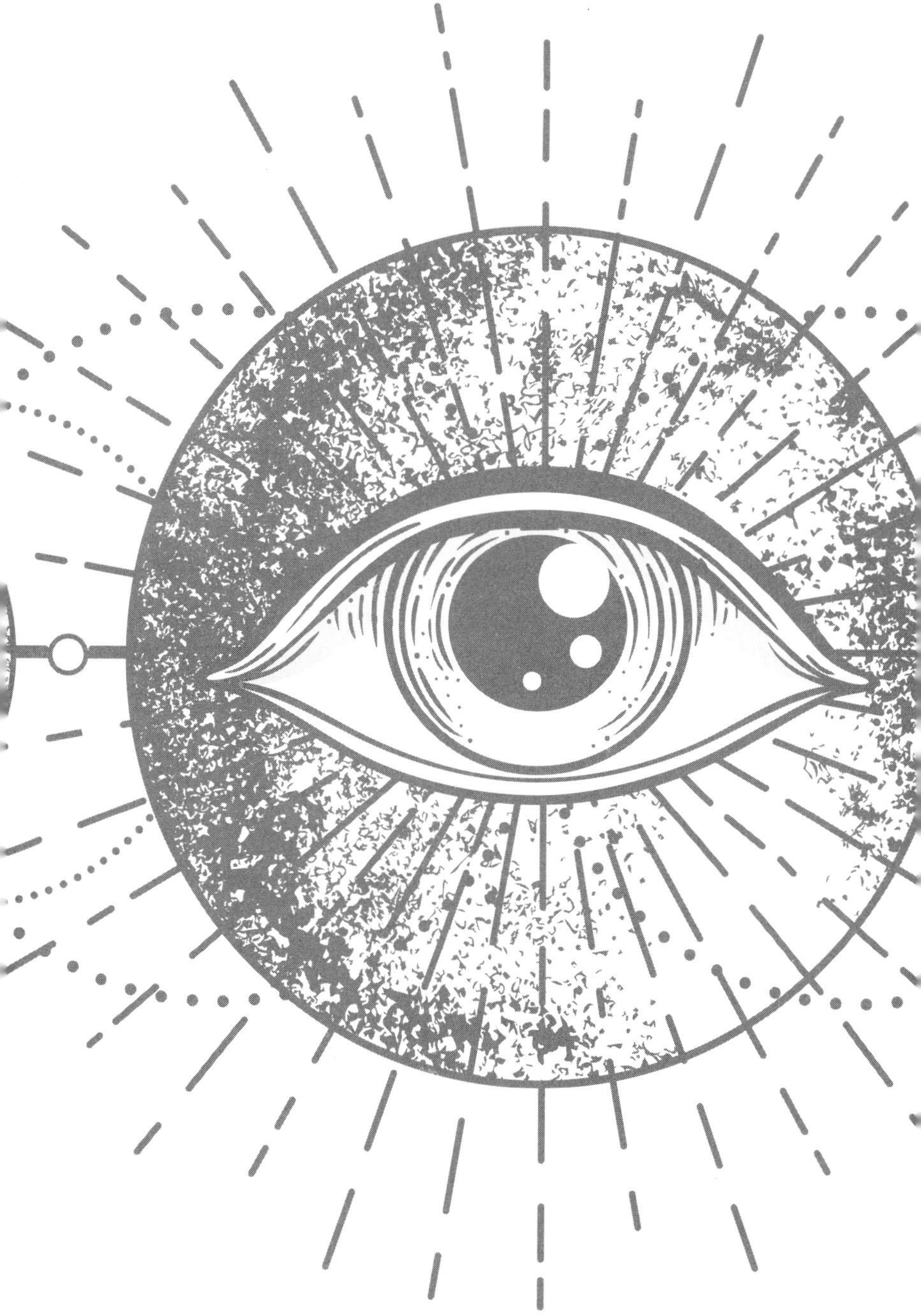

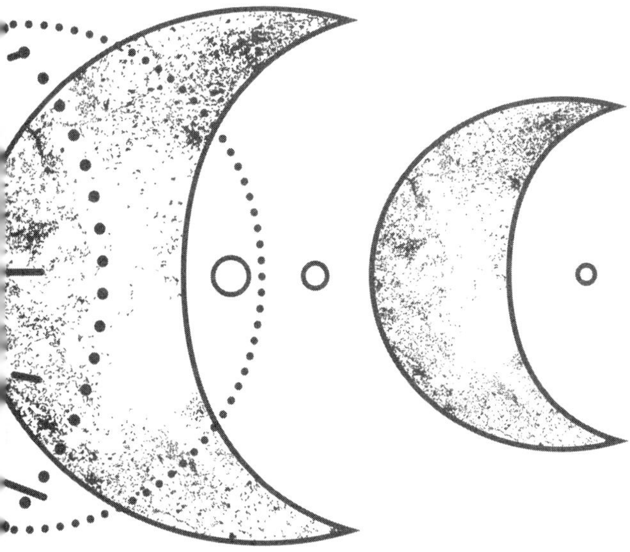

CATHARSIS

ABOUT THE PUBLISHER

Di Angelo Publications was founded in 2008 by Sequoia Schmidt—at the age of seventeen. The modernized publishing firm's creative headquarters is in Houston, Texas, with its distribution center located in Twin Falls, Idaho. The subsidiary rights department is based in Los Angeles, and Di Angelo Publications has recently grown to include branches in England, Australia, and Sequoia's home country of New Zealand. In 2020, Di Angelo Publications made a conscious decision to move all printing and production for domestic distribution of its books to the United States. The firm is comprised of eight imprints, and the featured imprint, Catharsis, was inspired by Schmidt's love of extreme sports, travel, and adventure stories.

DI ANGELO PUBLICATIONS

A Modernized Publishing Firm